Core Connections, Course 1
Toolkit

Managing Editors / Authors

Leslie Dietiker, Ph.D.
Boston University
Boston, MA

Evra Baldinger (First Edition)
University of California, Berkeley
Berkeley, CA

Michael Kassarjian (Second Edition)
CPM Educational Program
Kensington, CA

Barbara Shreve (First Edition)
San Lorenzo High School
San Lorenzo, CA

Misty Nikula (Second Edition)
CPM Educational Program
Bellingham, WA

Technical Assistants

Hannah Coyner
Sacramento, CA

Carmen de la Cruz
Davis, CA

Sarah Maile
Sacramento, CA

Cover Art

Jonathan Weast
Sacramento, CA

Program Directors

Leslie Dietiker, Ph.D.
Boston University
Boston, MA

Lori Hamada
CPM Educational Program
Fresno, CA

Brian Hoey
CPM Educational Program
Sacramento, CA

Judy Kysh, Ph.D.
Departments of Education and Mathematics
San Francisco State University, CA

Tom Sallee, Ph.D.
Department of Mathematics
University of California, Davis

9 10 11 12   21 20 19 18

Printed in the United States of America   ISBN: 978-1-60328-094-5

Core Connections, Course 1
Toolkit

Chapter 3 Portions and Integers 17

Chapter 4 Variables and Ratios 27

Dear Math Student,

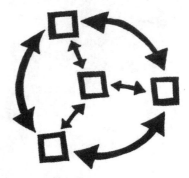

Welcome to your *Core Connections, Course 1* Toolkit! It is designed to help you as you learn math throughout the school year. Inside, you will find all of the Math Notes from your textbook that have useful information about the topics you will study. You will also be able to write in your Toolkit so that you can keep track of what you have learned in your own words and refer back to those notes as you move forward.

Many lessons in your math book include a prompt that asks you to think and write about the topic you are learning that day in a Learning Log. There is space in this Toolkit to write your Learning Log entries so that they are all in one place and are easy to use later. It is a good idea to leave some space between your entries so that you can add new ideas to them later, as you learn more. Note that this space has a light grid, which you can use like lined paper, as well as to help you draw diagrams or graphs.

Throughout the year, remember to make notes in your Toolkit and add examples if you find them helpful. It is important that the information on these pages—especially the Math Notes—makes sense to *you*, so be sure to highlight key information, write down important things to remember, and ask questions if something does not make sense.

Also remember that the information in your Toolkit can help you solve problems and keep track of important vocabulary words. Keep your Toolkit with you when you are working on math problems, and use it as a source of information as you move through the course.

At the end of each chapter in your textbook, there are lists of all of the Learning Log entries and Math Notes for that chapter. There are also lists of important vocabulary words. Take time as you complete each chapter to look through your Toolkit and make sure it is complete. Updating your Toolkit regularly and using it when you are studying are important student habits that will help you to be successful in this and future courses.

Have a wonderful year of learning!

The CPM Team

CHAPTER 1: INTRODUCTION AND REPRESENTATION

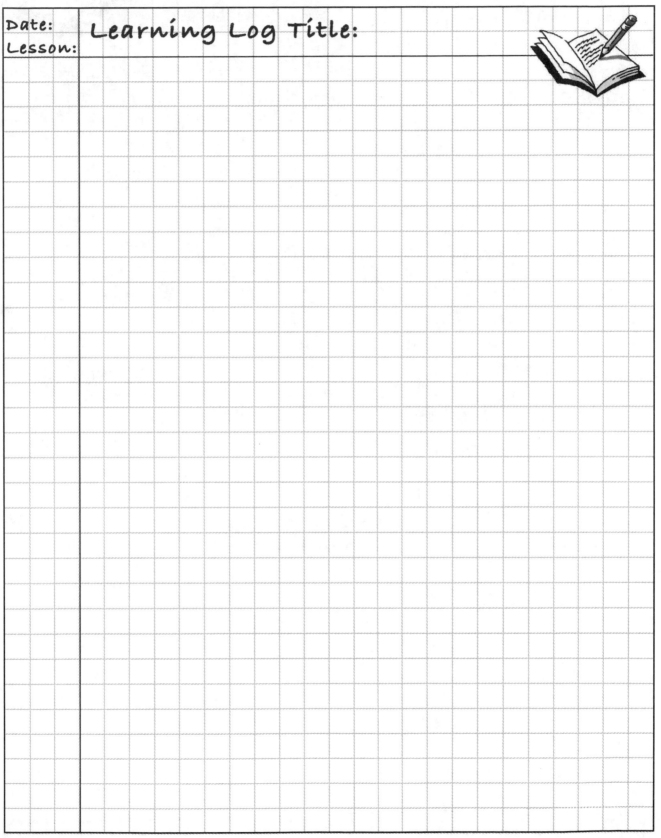

Date: Lesson:	Learning Log Title:

Date: Lesson:	Learning Log Title:

Date:	Learning Log Title:
Lesson:	

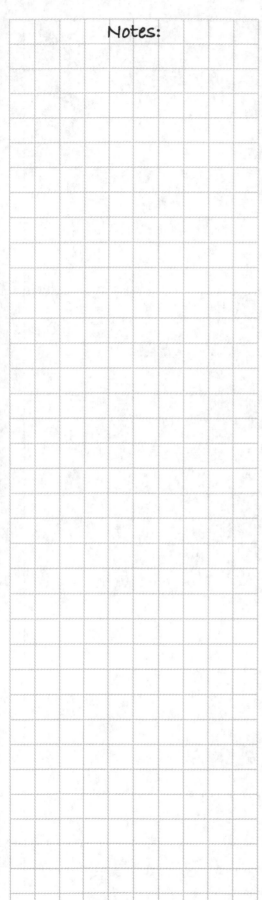

MATH NOTES

PERIMETER AND AREA

The **perimeter** of a shape is the total
length of the boundary (around the shape)
that encloses the interior (inside) region
on a flat surface. In the game "Toothpicks
and Tiles," the number of tile side lengths
(toothpicks) is the same as the **perimeter**
of the shape. See the examples at right.

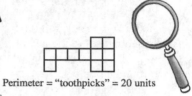

Perimeter = "toothpicks" = 20 units

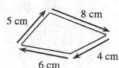

Perimeter = 5 + 8 + 4 + 6 = 23 cm

The **area** of a shape is a measure of the
number of square units needed to cover a
region on a flat surface. In the game, the
area is equal to the number of "tiles" in the
shape.

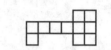

Area = "tiles" = 11 sq. units

A **rectangle** is a quadrilateral (four sides)
with four right angles. The opposite sides
are equal in length. Two sides that come
together (meet) at a right angle are
referred to as the length and width, or base
and height. The area (A) of any rectangle
is found by the relationship
A = length · width.

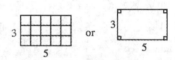

Base = 5, Height = 3
Area = 5 · 3 = 15 square units

PLACE VALUE

The number assigned to each place that a digit occupies is
called the **place value**. In our number system, the place values
are all powers of ten.

Starting from the left side of the decimal point, the place values are: ones,
tens, hundreds, thousands, ten thousands, and so on.

On the right side, the place values are ten**ths**, hundred**ths**, thousand**ths**,
and so on.

In the example at right, the
place occupied by 8 has the
value of 100, so the value of
the digit 8 is 800.

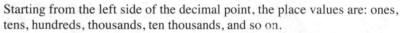

The number at right is read,
*"nine thousand, eight hundred
seventy-six and five hundred forty-three thousandths."*

The number 64.3 is read, *"sixty-four and three tenths."*

The number 7.17 is read, *"seven and seventeen hundredths."*

The only time the word *"and"* is said when reading a number is at the
location of the decimal point.

ROUNDING

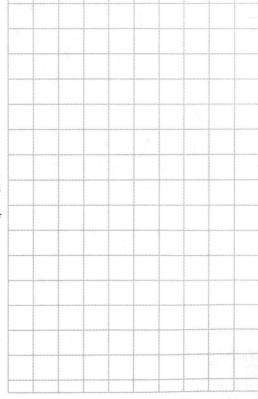

Sometimes you want an approximation of a number. One way to do this is to **round** the number. For example, 4,738 is 5,000 when rounded to thousands. The number 5,000 is said to be rounded "to the nearest thousand."

To round a number:
1. Find the place to which the number will be rounded.
2. Examine the digit one place to the right.
3. If the digit is 5 or greater, add 1 to the place you are rounding. If the digit is less than 5, keep the digit in the place you are rounding the same.

In the example 4738, the number 4 is in the thousands place. If you check the hundreds place, you see that 7 is greater than 5. This means the 4 needs to be increased by 1. Here are some other examples:

Round 431.6271 to the nearest tenth.
(1) Focus on the 6 in the tenths place.
(2) The number to the right (in the hundredths place) is 2. This is less than 5.
(3) 431.6 is the answer.

Round 17,389 to the nearest hundred.
(1) Focus on the 3 in the hundreds place.
(2) The number to the right (in the tens place) is 8. This is more than 5.
(3) 17,400 is the answer.

CONJECTURE AND JUSTIFY

A **conjecture** is a statement that appears to be true. It is an educated guess.

To **justify** a conjecture is to give reasons why your conjecture makes sense. In this course you will justify conjectures by using observations of a pattern, an algebraic validation, or some other logical method.

Notes:

Notes:

COMPARISONS

Mathematical symbols are used to compare quantities. The most commonly used symbols are the two inequality signs (< and >) and the equal sign (=). You can see how these symbols are used below.

greater than: >	$7 > 5$
less than: <	$3 < 5$
equal to: =	$1 + 2 = 3$
greater than or equal to: ≥	$4 \geq 4$
less than or equal to: ≤	$8 \leq 9$

NATURAL, WHOLE, AND PRIME NUMBERS

The numbers $\{1, 2, 3, 4, 5, 6, ...\}$ are called **natural numbers** or **counting numbers**. A natural number is **even** if it is divisible by two with no remainder. Otherwise the natural number is **odd**. The **whole numbers** include the natural numbers and zero.

If one natural number divides another without remainder, the first one is called a **factor** of the second. For example, the factors of 12 are 1, 2, 3, 4, 6, and 12. If a number has exactly two factors (1 and itself), it is called a **prime number**. If a number has more than two factors it is called a **composite number**. The number 1 has only one factor, so it is neither prime nor composite.

The prime numbers less than 40 are: 2, 3, 5, 7, 11, 13, 17, 19, 23, 29, 31, and 37.

CHAPTER 2: ARITHMETIC STRATEGIES AND AREA

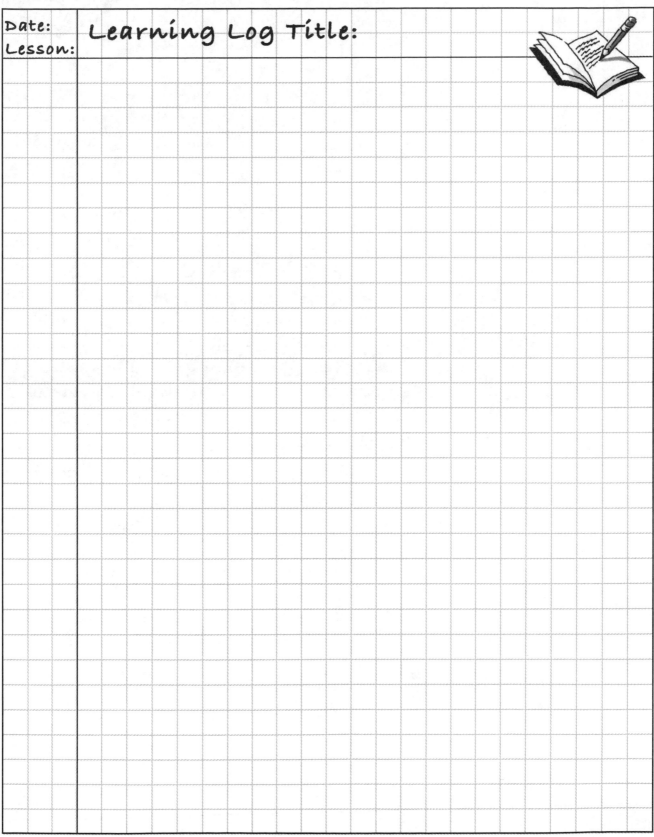

Date: Lesson:	Learning Log Title:

Date: Lesson:	Learning Log Title:

Date: Lesson:	Learning Log Title:

| Date: | Learning Log Title: |
| Lesson: | |

Date: Lesson:	Learning Log Title:

MATH NOTES

DISPLAYS OF DATA

Data can be displayed visually in different formats depending on the kind of information collected.

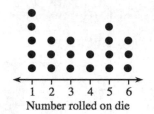

Number rolled on die

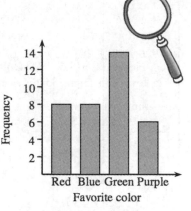

Favorite color

A **dot plot** is a way of displaying data that has an order and can be placed on a number line. Dot plots are generally used when the data is discrete (separate and distinct) and numerous pieces of data fall on most values. Examples: the number of siblings each student in your class has, the number of correct answers on a quiz, or the number rolled on a die (the graph above shows 20 rolls).

A **bar graph** is used when data falls in categories that typically have no numerical order. The graph above right shows that green is the favorite color of 14 students.

A **Venn diagram** is two or more overlapping circles used to show overlap between categories of data. The diagram at right shows that 7 students have both dogs and cats, 9 students have only dogs, 10 have only cats, 3 students do not have a dog or a cat, 16 students have dogs, and 17 students have cats.

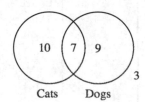

Cats   Dogs

HISTOGRAMS

A **histogram** is similar to a dot plot except that each bar represents data in an interval of numbers. The intervals for the data are shown on the horizontal axis. The frequency (number of pieces of data in each interval) is represented by the height of a bar above the interval. Each interval is also called a **bin**.

The labels on the horizontal axis represent the lower end of each interval. For example, the histogram at right shows that 10 students take at least 15 minutes but less than 30 minutes to get to school.

Histograms and dot plots are for displaying numeric data with an order. Bar graphs are for data in categories where order generally does not matter.

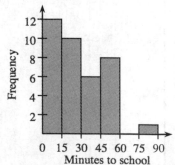

Minutes to school

Core Connections, Course 1

STEM-AND-LEAF PLOTS

A **stem-and-leaf plot** is similar to a histogram except that it shows the individual values from a set of data and how the values are distributed. The "stem" part of the graph represents all of the digits in a number except the last one. The "leaf" part of the graph represents the last digit of each of the numbers. Every stem-and-leaf plot needs a "key." The place value of the entries is determined by the key. This is important because 8|2 could mean 82 or 8.2.

Example: Students in a math class received the following scores on their tests: 49, 52, 54, 58, 61, 61, 67, 68, 72, 73, 73, 73, 78, 82, and 83. Display the test-score data on a stem-and-leaf plot.

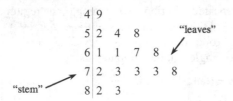

4	9
5	2 4 8
6	1 1 7 8
7	2 3 3 3 8
8	2 3

"leaves"

"stem"

```
Key
8|2   means "82"
```

AREA

The area of a region is the number of square units of the interior of a region. In this course, you will be asked to consider the area of flat regions (known as plane figures), such as the top of a table, the floor of your classroom, other various geometric shapes, or the surface of a pond.

To measure the area of a region, be sure to remember these important points:

- Any square can be used as a unit of area—a square inch, a square sticky note, a square centimeter, the square face of a block—but depending on the object being measured, some units are more convenient and common than others.
- To determine the area of a region, count the number of square units that are needed to cover the region completely without gaps or overlaps.
- If the square units you have chosen do not fit exactly within the region boundaries, you will have to find a way to determine what part of the square units are needed.
- When the answer is stated, be sure to include the kind of square units that are being used.

Example: In the sample figures below, assume each small square is one square centimeter and estimate the area of each figure.

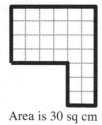

Area is 30 sq cm

Area is between 23 and 24 sq cm

AREA, RECTANGLES, AND SQUARE UNITS

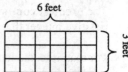

To find the **area of a rectangle**, choose a conveniently sized square unit to cover the rectangle exactly with no overlaps. Sometimes parts of square units are needed to cover the rectangle completely.

In the rectangle at right, using squares with side lengths of one foot, it takes 18 squares to cover the rectangle. Therefore, the area of the rectangle is 18 square feet.

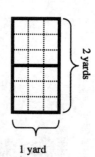

One way to count squares in a rectangle quickly is to multiply the lengths of two sides that meet (intersect) at a corner, since multiplication is defined as repeated addition. For example, the region of the rectangle above can be seen as either six groups of three squares (viewed as columns) or three groups of six squares (viewed as rows). In either case, the area of a rectangle can be computed using:

$$A = (\text{length})(\text{width})$$

The same-sized shape may appear to have different areas if it is measured using different units of measure. Of course, the area did not change, but the number of different-sized units did. Note that the rectangle shown at right is the same size as the one above, but it is measured in yards instead of feet. The top rectangle has an area of 18 square feet. The area of the rectangle at right has an area of 2 square yards.

Units for area can be abbreviated using symbols. The area 18 square feet is abbreviated 18 sq ft or 18 ft^2. The area 2 square yards is abbreviated 2 sq yd or 2 yd^2.

MULTIPLICATION USING GENERIC RECTANGLES

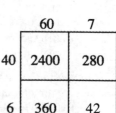

To prepare for later topics in this course and future courses it is helpful to use an area model or generic rectangle to represent multiplication.

For the problem $67 \cdot 46$, think of 67 as $60 + 7$ and 46 as $40 + 6$. Use these numbers as the dimensions of a large rectangle as shown at right. Determine the area of each of the smaller rectangles and then find the sum of the four smaller areas. This sum is the answer to the original problem.

	60	7
40	2400	280
6	360	42

$$67 \cdot 46 = (60 + 7)(40 + 6) = 2400 + 280 + 360 + 42 = 3082$$

GREATEST COMMON FACTOR

To find the **area of a rectangle**, choose a conveniently sized square unit to cover the rectangle exactly with no overlaps. Sometimes parts of square units are needed to completely cover the rectangle.

The **greatest common factor** of two or more integers is the greatest positive integer that is a factor of both (or all) of the integers.

For example, the factors of 18 are 1, 2, 3, 6, and 18 and the factors of 12 are 1, 2, 3, 4, 6, and 12, so the greatest common factor of 12 and 18 is 6.

DISTRIBUTIVE PROPERTY

The **Distributive Property** states that the multiplier of a sum or difference can be "distributed" to multiply each term. For example to multiply 8(24), written as 8(20 + 4), you can use the generic-rectangle model below.

The product is found by 8(20) + 8(4).
So 8(20 + 4) = 8(20) + 8(4).

	20	+ 4
8	$8 \cdot 20$	$8 \cdot 4$

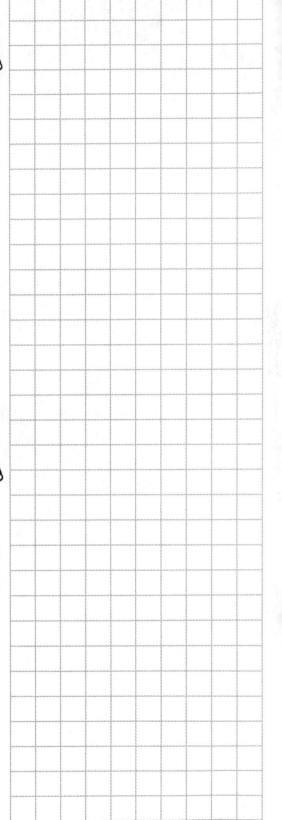

Notes:

CHAPTER 3: PORTIONS AND INTEGERS

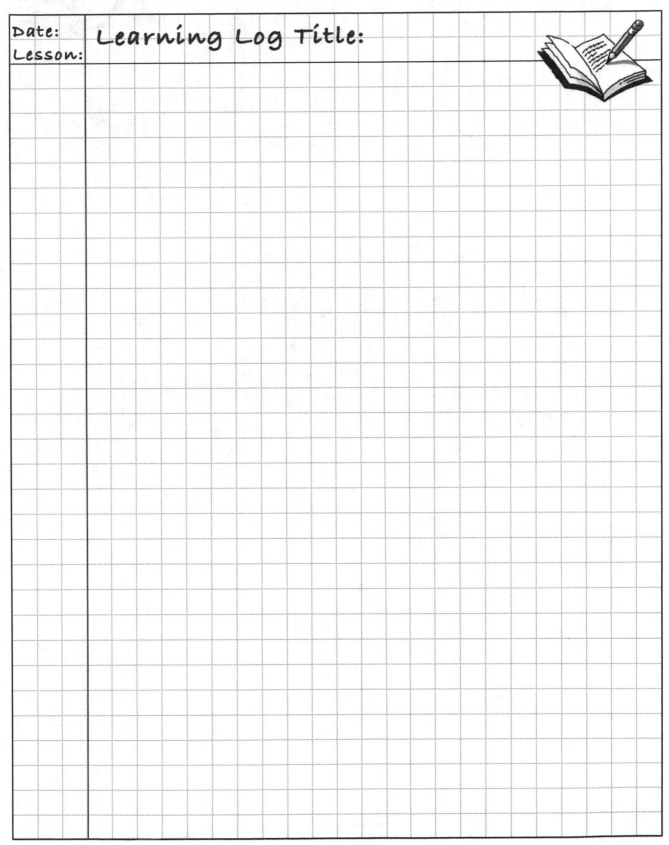

Date: Lesson:	Learning Log Title:

Date:	Learning Log Title:
Lesson:	

Date:	Learning Log Title:
Lesson:	

Date:	Learning Log Title:
Lesson:	

MATH NOTES

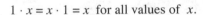

MULTIPLICATIVE IDENTITY

If any number or expression is multiplied by the number 1, the result is equal to the original number or expression. The number 1 is called the **multiplicative identity**. Formally, the identity is written:

$1 \cdot x = x \cdot 1 = x$ for all values of x.

One way the multiplicative identity is used is to create equivalent fractions using a Giant One.

$$\frac{2}{3} \cdot \boxed{\frac{2}{2}} = \frac{4}{6}$$

Multiplying any fraction by a Giant One will create a new fraction equivalent to the original fraction.

ADDING AND SUBTRACTING FRACTIONS

To add or subtract two fractions that are written with the same denominator (the number on the bottom), simply add or subtract the numerators (the numbers on the top). For example, $\frac{1}{5} + \frac{2}{5} = \frac{3}{5}$.

If the fractions have different denominators, **rewrite them first** as fractions with the same denominator. (One way to do this is to use a Giant One.) Below are examples of adding and subtracting two fractions with different denominators.

Addition example: $\frac{1}{5} + \frac{2}{3} \Rightarrow \frac{1}{5} \cdot \boxed{\frac{3}{3}} + \frac{2}{3} \cdot \boxed{\frac{5}{5}} \Rightarrow \frac{3}{15} + \frac{10}{15} = \frac{13}{15}$

Subtraction example: $\frac{5}{6} - \frac{1}{4} \Rightarrow \frac{5}{6} \cdot \boxed{\frac{2}{2}} - \frac{1}{4} \cdot \boxed{\frac{3}{3}} \Rightarrow \frac{10}{12} - \frac{3}{12} = \frac{7}{12}$

Using algebra to write the general method: $\frac{a}{b} + \frac{c}{d} \Rightarrow \frac{a}{b} \cdot \boxed{\frac{d}{d}} + \frac{c}{d} \cdot \boxed{\frac{b}{b}} \Rightarrow \frac{a \cdot d}{b \cdot d} + \frac{b \cdot c}{b \cdot d} \Rightarrow \frac{a \cdot d + b \cdot c}{b \cdot d}$

100% BLOCKS

Base Ten Blocks can also be used to represent percents. The three basic blocks represent 100%, 10%, and 1% as shown at right.

A **percent** is a way of expressing a number as a fraction out of 100. In the example shown at right, 23 out of 100 squares are shaded to represent 23%. 23% can be expressed as $\frac{23}{100}$, 0.23, or twenty-three hundredths.

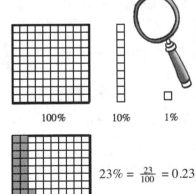

100%   10%   1%

$23\% = \frac{23}{100} = 0.23$

Notes:

PERCENTS

A percent is one way to write a portion of 100. It can always be written as a fraction with a denominator of 100 and/or as a decimal.

Commonly Used Percents

$$100\% = \frac{100}{100} = 1$$

$$75\% = \frac{75}{100} = \frac{3}{4} = 0.75$$

$$50\% = \frac{50}{100} = \frac{1}{2} = 0.5$$

$$25\% = \frac{25}{100} = \frac{1}{4} = 0.25$$

$$10\% = \frac{10}{100} = \frac{1}{10} = 0.1$$

$$1\% = \frac{1}{100} = 0.01$$

Useful Percents to Remember

$$80\% = \frac{80}{100} = \frac{4}{5} = 0.8$$

$$60\% = \frac{60}{100} = \frac{3}{5} = 0.6$$

$$40\% = \frac{40}{100} = \frac{2}{5} = 0.4$$

$$20\% = \frac{20}{100} = \frac{1}{5} = 0.2$$

$$33\tfrac{1}{3}\% = \frac{33\frac{1}{3}}{100} = \frac{1}{3} = 0.\overline{3}$$

$$66\tfrac{2}{3}\% = \frac{66\frac{2}{3}}{100} = \frac{2}{3} = 0.\overline{6}$$

Fraction ⇔ Decimal ⇔ Percent

The **Representations of a Portion web** diagram at right illustrates that fractions, decimals, and percents are different ways to represent a portion of a number. Portions can also be represented in words, such as "four fifths" or "twelve fifteenths" or with diagrams.

The examples below show how to convert from one form to another.

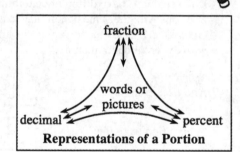

Representations of a Portion

Decimal to percent:
Multiply the decimal by 100.

$$(0.34)(100) = 34\%$$

Fraction to percent:
Set up an equivalent fraction using 100 as the denominator. The numerator is the percent.

$$\frac{4}{5} \cdot \frac{20}{20} = \frac{80}{100} = 80\%$$

Decimal to fraction:
Use the digits as the numerator. Use the decimal place value as the denominator. Simplify as needed.

$$0.2 = \frac{2}{10} = \frac{1}{5}$$

Percent to decimal:
Divide the percent by 100.

$$78.6\% = 78.6 \div 100 = 0.786$$

Percent to fraction:
Use 100 as the denominator. Use the number in the percent as the numerator. Simplify as needed.

$$22\% = \frac{22}{100} \cdot \frac{1/2}{1/2} = \frac{11}{50}$$

Fraction to decimal:
Divide the numerator by the denominator.

$$\frac{3}{8} = 3 \div 8 = 0.375$$

GRAPHING POINTS ON AN *XY*-COORDINATE GRAPH

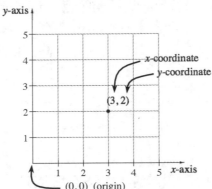

Numerical data that you want to put on a two-dimensional graph is entered on the graph as **points**.

The graph has a horizontal number line, called the ***x*-axis**, and a vertical number line, called the ***y*-axis**. The two axes cross at the **origin** $(0, 0)$ which is the 0 point on each axis.

Points on the graph are identified by two numbers in an **ordered pair**. An ordered pair is written as (x, y). The first number is the ***x*-coordinate** of the point and the second number is the ***y*-coordinate**.

To locate the point $(3, 2)$ on an *xy*-graph, first start at the origin. Go 3 units to the right (to the mark 3 on the horizontal axis). Then, from that point, go 2 units up (to the mark across from 2 on the vertical axis).

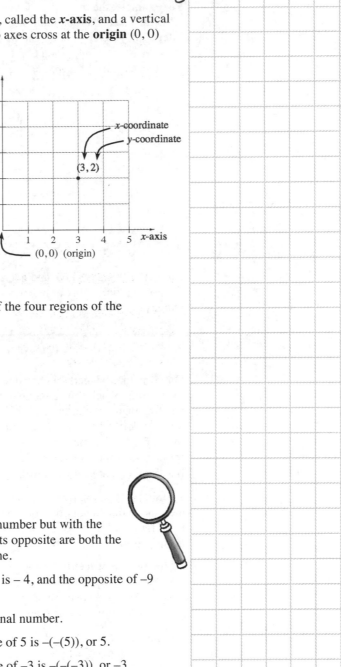

The example graph above shows one of the four regions of the *xy*-coordinate graph.

OPPOSITES

The **opposite** of a number is the same number but with the opposite sign (+ or –). A number and its opposite are both the same distance from 0 on the number line.

For example, the opposite of 4 (or + 4) is – 4, and the opposite of –9 is –(–9) = 9 (or +9).

The opposite of an opposite is the original number.

Examples: The opposite of the opposite of 5 is –(–(5)), or 5.

The opposite of the opposite of –3 is –(–(–3)), or –3.

The opposite of zero is zero.

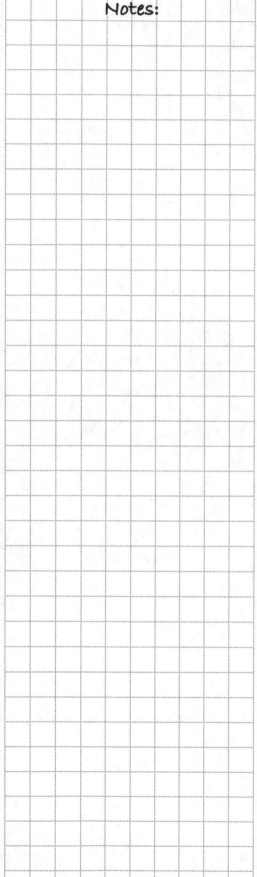

LEAST COMMON MULTIPLE

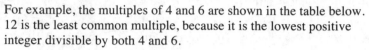

The **least common multiple** (LCM) of two or more positive or negative whole numbers is the lowest positive whole number that is divisible by both (or all) of the numbers.

For example, the multiples of 4 and 6 are shown in the table below. 12 is the least common multiple, because it is the lowest positive integer divisible by both 4 and 6.

4	8	**12**	16	20	24	28	32
6	**12**	18	24	30	36	42	48

ADDING INTEGERS

Integers are the positive and negative whole numbers and zero. On the number line, think of integers as "whole steps or no steps" in either direction from 0.

One way that integers can be combined is by **adding**, which can be thought of as walking on a number line. If you walk one step left (−1), and then one step back to the right (+1), you end up in the same place as you started. This is represented on the number line as −1 + 1 = 0. A number and its opposite, like 5 and −5, are called **additive inverses**, and their sum is zero (0).

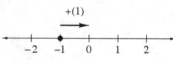

To **add integers** on a number line, mark the position of the first integer, and then move the number of units indicated by the second integer. Move to the right for positive integers and move to the left for negative integers. Examples are provided below.

Example 1: −5 + (2) = −3

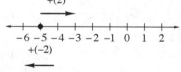

Example 2: −6 + (−2) = −8

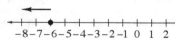

ABSOLUTE VALUE

Absolute value represents the numerical value of a number without regard to its sign. Absolute value can represent the distance on a number line between a number and zero. The symbol for absolute value is two vertical bars, | |. For example:

$$|-3| = 3 \text{ and } |3| = 3$$

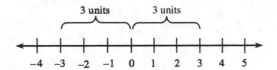

Notes:

CHAPTER 4: VARIABLES AND RATIOS

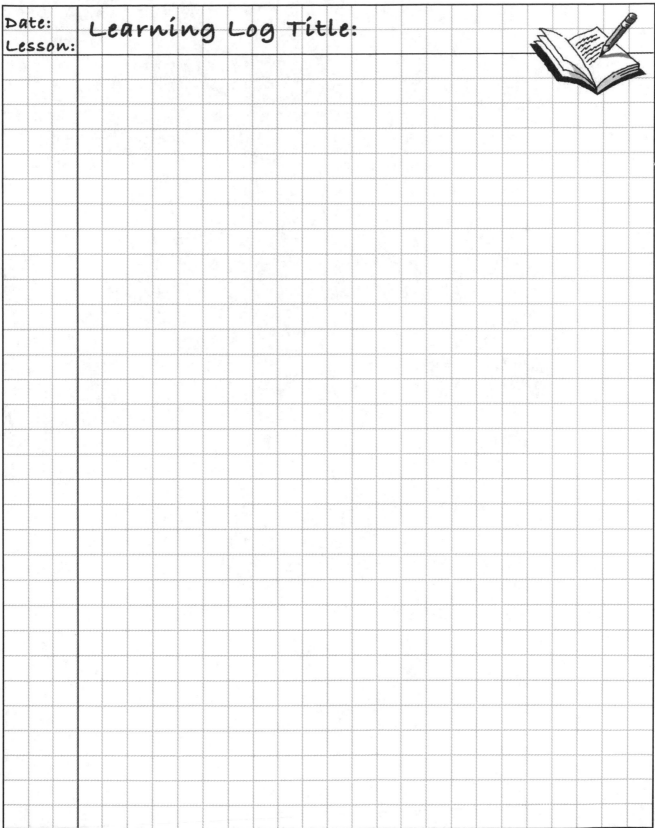

Date: Lesson:	Learning Log Title:

Date: Lesson:	Learning Log Title:

Date:
Lesson:

Learning Log Title:

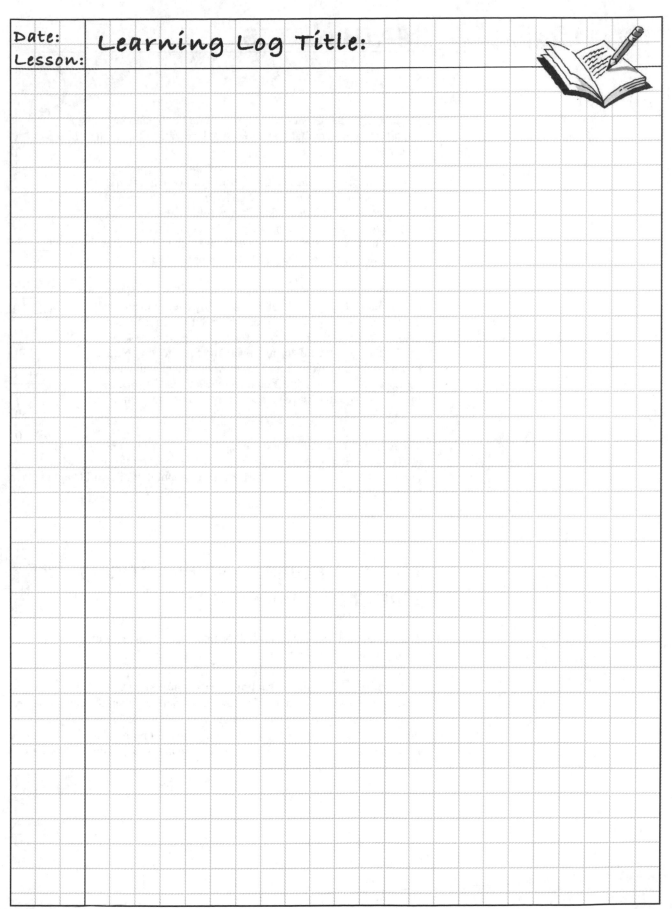

MATH NOTES

DIVIDING

When using long division to divide one number by another, it is important to be sure that you know the place value of each digit in your result.

$$\begin{array}{r} 37 \\ 6\overline{)225} \\ -180 \\ \hline 45 \\ -42 \\ \hline 3 \end{array}$$

In the example of dividing 225 by 6 at right, people often begin by saying, *"6 goes into 22 three times."* If they were paying attention to place value, they would instead say *"6 goes into 220 thirty-something times."* The 3 of the quotient is written in the tens place to indicate that 6 goes into 225 at least 30 times, but less than 40. The 3 represents 3 tens.

It may seem like the divisor is then multiplied by the 3, and the product, 18, is placed below a 22. However, you are really multiplying 30 by 6 and the product is 180, which is placed below 225. You would then subtract, getting what looks like 4. But then you would "bring down" the 5, to get 45. Notice that if you subtract 180 from 225, as in the top example at right, you get 45 directly. You then repeat the same process. In the past, you may have stopped at this point and written that the quotient is 37 with a remainder of 3.

$$\begin{array}{r} 37.5 \\ 6\overline{)225.0} \\ -180 \\ \hline 45 \\ -42 \\ \hline 30 \\ 30 \\ \hline 0 \end{array}$$

The same method works for dividing decimals. The second example above is essentially the same as the top one, except that it shows what happens if you keep dividing past the decimal point, while still keeping place value in mind.

MIXED NUMBERS AND FRACTIONS GREATER THAN ONE

The number $3\frac{1}{4}$ is called a **mixed number** because it is composed of a whole number, 3, and a fraction, $\frac{1}{4}$.

The number $\frac{13}{4}$ is called a **fraction greater than one** because the numerator, which represents the number of equal pieces, is larger than the denominator, which represents the number of pieces in one whole, so its value is greater than one. (Sometimes such fractions are called "improper fractions," but this is just a historical term. There is nothing actually wrong with the fractions.)

As you can see in the diagram at right, the fraction $\frac{13}{4}$ can be rewritten as $\frac{4}{4}+\frac{4}{4}+\frac{4}{4}+\frac{1}{4}$, which shows that it is equal in value to $3\frac{1}{4}$.

Your choice: Depending on which arithmetic operations you need to perform, you will choose whether to write your number as a mixed number or as a fraction greater than one.

ADDING AND SUBTRACTING MIXED NUMBERS

To **add or subtract mixed numbers**, you can either add or subtract their parts, or you can change the mixed numbers into fractions greater than one.

To add or subtract mixed numbers by adding or subtracting their parts, add or subtract the whole-number parts and the fraction parts separately.

$$3\frac{4}{5} = 3 + \frac{4}{5} \cdot \boxed{\frac{3}{3}} = 3\frac{12}{15}$$
$$+1\frac{2}{3} = 1 + \frac{2}{3} \cdot \boxed{\frac{5}{5}} = +1\frac{10}{15}$$
$$4\frac{22}{15} = 5\frac{7}{15}$$

Adjust if the fraction in the answer would be greater than one or less than zero. For example, the sum of $3\frac{4}{5} + 1\frac{2}{3}$ is calculated at right above.

It is also possible to add or subtract mixed numbers by first changing them into fractions greater than one. Then add or subtract in the same way you would if they were fractions between 0 and 1. For example, the sum of $2\frac{1}{6} + 1\frac{4}{5}$ is calculated at right.

$$2\frac{1}{6} + 1\frac{4}{5} = \frac{13}{6} + \frac{9}{5}$$
$$= \frac{13}{6} \cdot \boxed{\frac{5}{5}} + \frac{9}{5} \cdot \boxed{\frac{6}{6}}$$
$$= \frac{65}{30} + \frac{54}{30}$$
$$= \frac{119}{30}$$
$$= 3\frac{29}{30}$$

USING VARIABLES TO GENERALIZE

Variables are letters or symbols used to represent one or more numbers. They are often used to generalize patterns from a few specific numbers to include all possible numbers.

For example, if a square is surrounded by smaller square tiles each measuring one centimeter on a side, how many tiles are needed? It helps to look at a specific of size square first.

The outside square at right has side length 7. One way to see the total number of tiles needed for the frame is to consider that it needs 7 tiles for each of the top and bottom sides and $7 - 2 = 5$ tiles for the left and right sides. This is shown in the first diagram at right. The total number of tiles needed for the frame can be counted as $7 + 7 + 5 + 5 = 24$.

Square frames with different side lengths will follow the same pattern. You can generalize by writing an expression for any side length, denoted by x. The second diagram at right shows that the top and bottom each contain x tiles. The right and left sides each contain $x - 2$ tiles. You could write the total number of tiles as either $x + x + (x - 2) + (x - 2)$, $2x + 2(x - 2)$, or even as $4x - 4$.

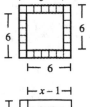

Shown at right are two additional square-frame diagrams. The diagram on the left shows another way to count the number of tiles in a frame. The diagram on the right shows the algebraic expression associated with it. Notice that the expression resulting from this counting method could be written $(x - 1) + (x - 1) + (x - 1) + (x - 1)$, or $4(x - 1)$.

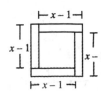

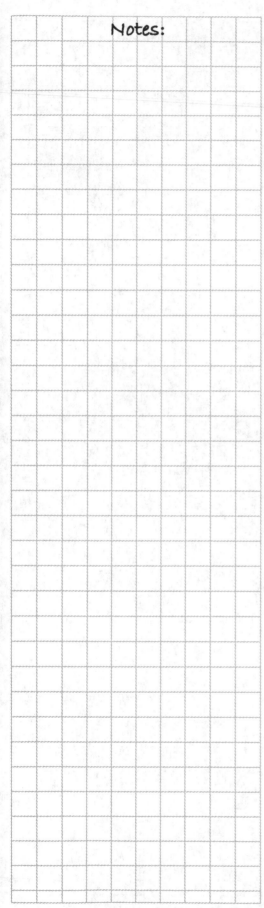

Notes:

EVALUATING ALGEBRAIC EXPRESSIONS

An **algebraic expression**, also known as a *variable expression*, is a combination of numbers and variables, connected by mathematical operations. For example, $4x$, $3(x - 5)$, and $4x - 3y + 7$ are algebraic expressions.

Addition and subtraction separate expressions into parts called **terms**. For example the expression above, $4x - 3y + 7$, has three terms: $4x$, $-3y$, and 7.

A more complex expression is $2x + 3(5 - 2x) + 8$. It also has three terms: $2x$, $3(5 - 2x)$, and 8. But the term $3(5 - 2x)$ has another expression, $5 - 2x$, inside the parentheses. The terms of this inner expression are 5 and $-2x$.

To **evaluate** an algebraic expression for particular values of variables, replace the variables in the expression with their known numerical values and simplify. Replacing variables with their known values is called **substitution**. An example is provided below.

Evaluate $4x - 3y + 7$ for $x = 2$ and $y = 1$.

Replace x and y with their known values of 2 and 1, respectively, and simplify.

$$4(2) - 3(1) + 7$$
$$8 - 3 + 7$$
$$12$$

RATIOS

A **ratio** is a comparison of two numbers, often written as a quotient; that is, the first number is divided by the second number (but not zero). A ratio can be written in words, in fraction form, or with colon notation. Most often, in this class, you will either write ratios in the form of fractions or state the ratios in words.

For example, if there are 38 students in a school band and 16 of them are boys, you can write the ratio of the number of boys to the number of girls as:

16 boys to 22 girls $\dfrac{16 \text{ boys}}{22 \text{ girls}}$ 16 boys : 22 girls

CHAPTER 5: MULTIPLYING FRACTIONS AND AREA

Date: Lesson:	Learning Log Title:

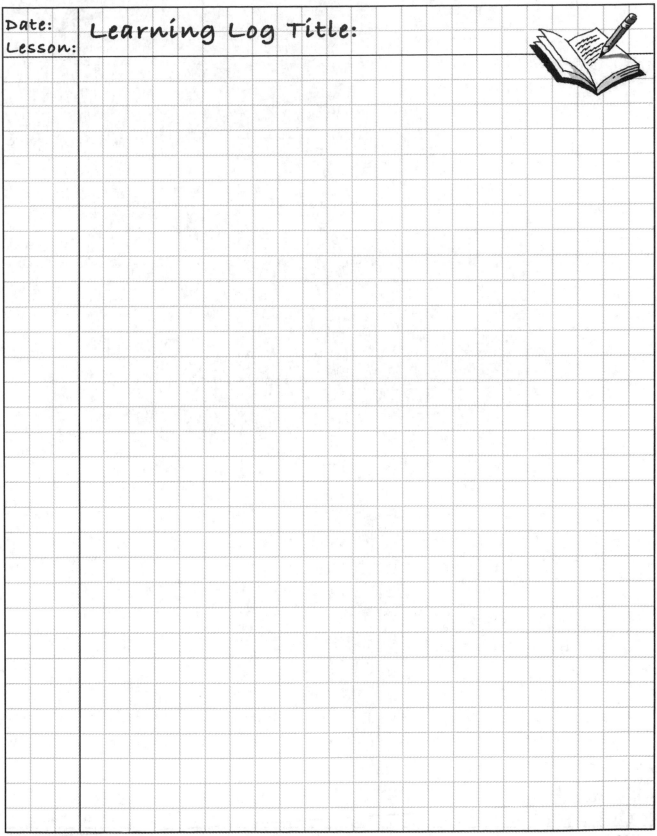

Date:	Learning Log Title:
Lesson:	

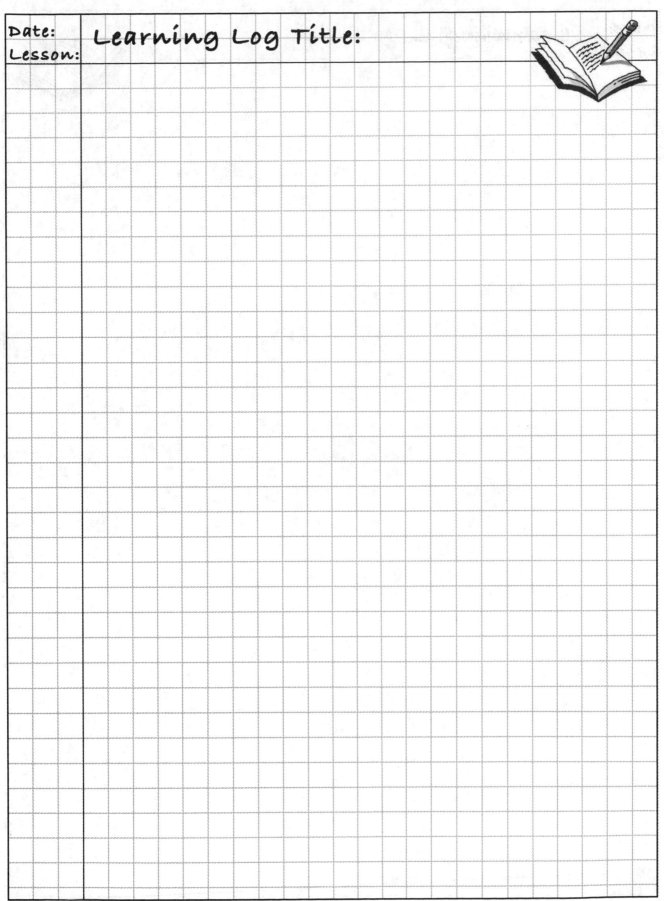

| Date: | Learning Log Title: |
| Lesson: | |

Date:	Learning Log Title:
Lesson:	

MATH NOTES

MULTIPLYING FRACTIONS

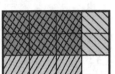

You can find the product of two fractions, such as $\frac{2}{3}$ and $\frac{3}{4}$, by multiplying the numerators (tops) of the fractions together and dividing that by the product of the denominators (bottoms). So $\frac{2}{3} \cdot \frac{3}{4} = \frac{6}{12}$, which is equivalent to $\frac{1}{2}$. Similarly, $\frac{4}{7} \cdot \frac{3}{5} = \frac{12}{35}$. If you write this method in algebraic terms, you would say $\frac{a}{b} \cdot \frac{c}{d} = \frac{a \cdot c}{b \cdot d}$.

The reason that this rule works can be seen using an area model of multiplication, as shown at right, which represents $\frac{2}{3} \cdot \frac{3}{4}$. The product of the denominators is the total number of smaller rectangles, while the product of the numerators is the number of the rectangles that are double-shaded.

MULTIPLYING MIXED NUMBERS

An efficient method for **multiplying mixed numbers** is to convert them to fractions greater than one, find the product as you would with fractions less than one, and then convert them back to a mixed number, if necessary. (Note that you may also use generic rectangles to find these products.) Here are three examples:

$$1\tfrac{2}{3} \cdot 2\tfrac{3}{4} = \tfrac{5}{3} \cdot \tfrac{11}{4} = \tfrac{55}{12} = 4\tfrac{7}{12} \qquad\qquad 1\tfrac{3}{5} \cdot \tfrac{2}{9} = \tfrac{8}{5} \cdot \tfrac{2}{9} = \tfrac{16}{45}$$

$$2\tfrac{1}{3} \cdot 4\tfrac{1}{2} = \tfrac{7}{3} \cdot \tfrac{9}{2} = \tfrac{63}{6} = 10\tfrac{3}{6} = 10\tfrac{1}{2}$$

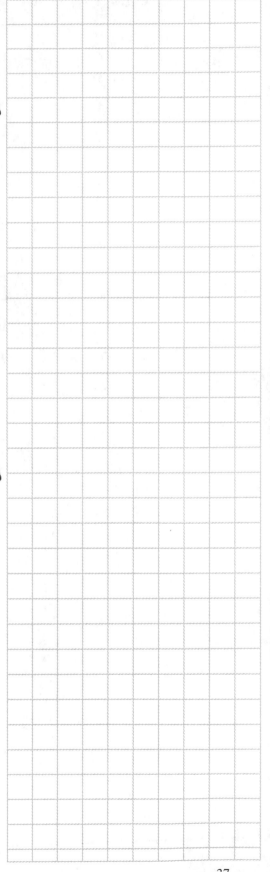

Notes:

MULTIPLYING DECIMALS

There are at least two ways to multiply decimals. One way is to convert the decimals to fractions and use your knowledge of fraction multiplication to compute the answer. The other way is to use the method that you have used to multiply integers; the only difference is that you need to keep track of where the decimal point is (place value) as you record each line of your work.

The examples below show how to compute 1.4(2.35) both ways by using generic rectangles.

	2	$\frac{3}{10}$	$\frac{5}{100}$
1	2	$\frac{3}{10}$	$\frac{5}{100}$
$\frac{4}{10}$	$\frac{8}{10}$	$\frac{12}{100}$	$\frac{20}{1000}$

	2	0.3	0.05
1	2	0.3	0.05
0.4	0.8	0.12	0.02

If you carried out the computation as shown above, you can calculate the product in either of the two ways shown at right. In the first one, you write down all of the values in the smaller rectangles within the generic rectangle and add the six numbers. In the second example, you combine the values in each row and then add the two rows. You usually write the answer as 3.29 since there are zero thousandths in the product.

$$
\begin{array}{r}
2.35 \\
\times \ 1.4 \\
\hline
0.020 \\
0.12 \\
0.8 \\
0.05 \\
0.3 \\
2.0 \\
\hline
3.290
\end{array}
$$

$$
\begin{array}{r}
2.35 \\
\times \ 1.4 \\
\hline
0.940 \\
2.35 \\
\hline
3.29
\end{array}
$$

BASE AND HEIGHT OF A RECTANGLE

Any side of a rectangle can be chosen as its **base**. Then the **height** is either of the two sides that intersect (meet) the base at one of its endpoints. Note that the height may also be any segment that is **perpendicular** to (each end forms a right angle (90°) with) both the base and the side opposite (across from) the base.

In the first rectangle at right, side $\overline{BC}$ is labeled as the base. Either side, $\overline{AB}$ or $\overline{DC}$, is a height, as is segment $\overline{FE}$.

In the second rectangle, side $\overline{GJ}$ is labeled as the base. Either side, $\overline{HG}$ or $\overline{IJ}$, is a height, as is segment $\overline{MN}$. Segment $\overline{GL}$ is not a height, because it is not perpendicular to side $\overline{GJ}$.

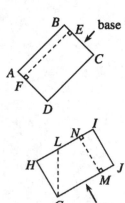

PARALLELOGRAM VOCABULARY

Two lines in a plane (a flat surface) are **parallel** if they never meet no matter how far they extend. The distance between the parallel lines is always the same. The marks " >> " indicate that the two lines are parallel.

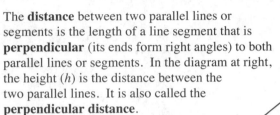

The **distance** between two parallel lines or segments is the length of a line segment that is **perpendicular** (its ends form right angles) to both parallel lines or segments. In the diagram at right, the height (h) is the distance between the two parallel lines. It is also called the **perpendicular distance**.

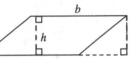

A **parallelogram** is a quadrilateral (a four-sided figure) with two pairs of parallel sides. Any side of a parallelogram can be used as a base. The height (h) is perpendicular to one of the pairs of parallel bases (b), or an extension of a base like the dashed line in the example at lower right.

AREA OF A PARALLELOGRAM

A parallelogram can be rearranged into a rectangle with the same base length and height. Since the area of a shape does not change when it is cut apart and its pieces are put together in a different arrangement (a principle called **conservation of area**), the area of the parallelogram must equal the product of its base and height.

Therefore, to find the area of a parallelogram, find the product of the length of the base (b) and the height (h).

$$A = b \cdot h$$

AREA OF A TRIANGLE

Since two copies of the same triangle can be put together along a common side to form a parallelogram with the same base and height as the triangle, then the **area of a triangle** must equal half the area of the parallelogram with the same base and height.

Therefore, if b is the base of a triangle and h is the height of the triangle, you can think of triangles as "half parallelograms" and calculate the area of any triangle:

$$A = \tfrac{1}{2} b \cdot h$$

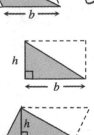

Notes:

CHAPTER 6: DIVIDING AND BUILDING EXPRESSIONS

Date: Lesson:	Learning Log Title:

Date:	Learning Log Title:
Lesson:	

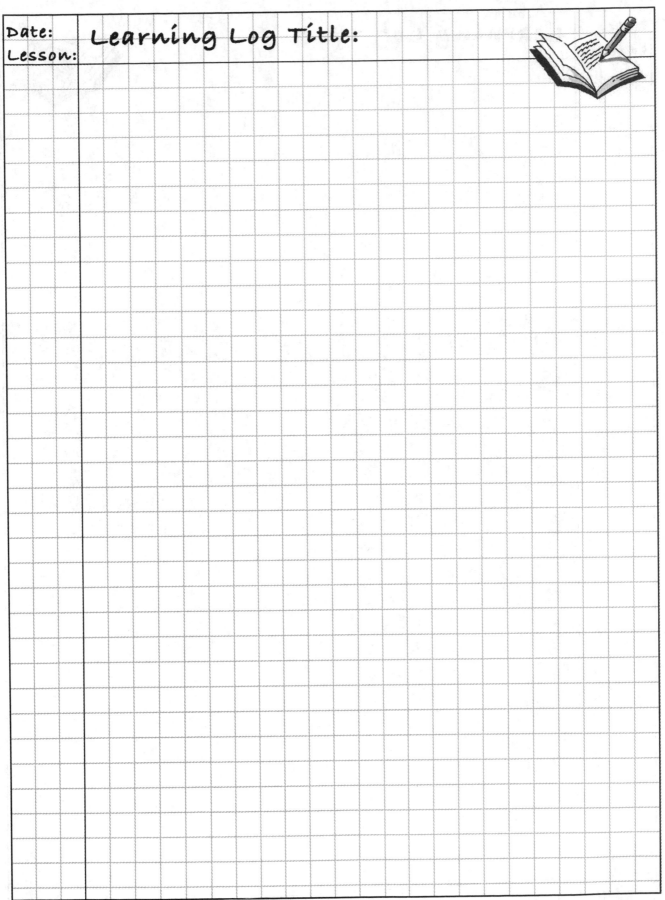

| Date:
Lesson: | Learning Log Title: |

Date:	Learning Log Title:
Lesson:	

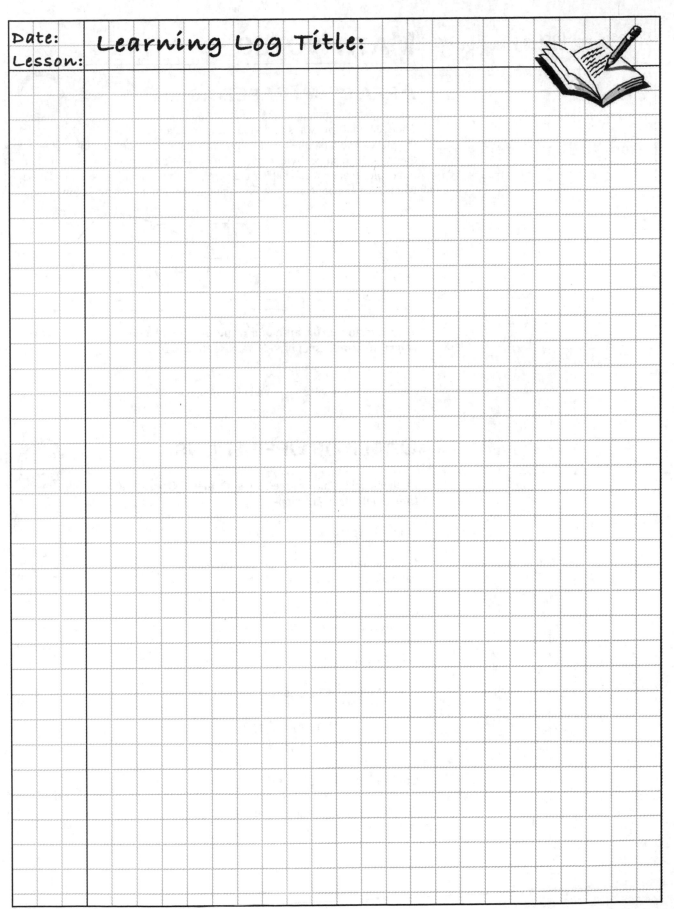

Date:
Lesson:

Learning Log Title:

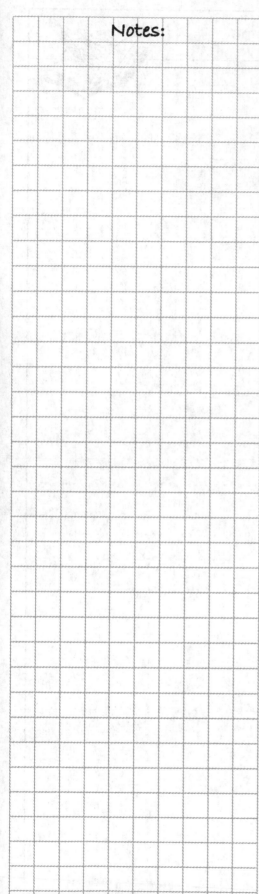

MATH NOTES

AREA OF A TRAPEZOID

There are multiple ways to divide a trapezoid and rearrange the pieces into a parallelogram with the same area. For example, the trapezoid can be divided parallel to its two bases to create two smaller trapezoids that are each half of the height of the original trapezoid. Those two pieces can be rearranged into a parallelogram, as shown below.

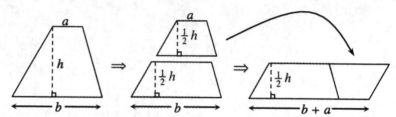

Therefore, to find the **area of a trapezoid**, find the product of half of the height (h) and the sum of the two bases (a and b).

$$A = \tfrac{1}{2}h(a+b)$$

ORDER OF OPERATIONS

Mathematicians have agreed on an **Order of Operations** for simplifying expressions.

Original expression:

$$(10 - 3 \cdot 2) \cdot 2^2 - \tfrac{13 - 3^2}{2} + 6$$

Circle expressions that are grouped within parentheses or by a fraction bar:

$$\boxed{(10 - 3 \cdot 2)} \cdot 2^2 - \frac{\boxed{13 - 3^2}}{2} + 6$$

Simplify *within* circled expressions using the Order of Operations:

- Evaluate exponents.

$$\boxed{(10 - 3 \cdot 2)} \cdot 2^2 - \frac{\boxed{13 - 3 \cdot 3}}{2} + 6$$

- Multiply and divide from left to right.

$$\boxed{(10 - 6)} \cdot 2^2 - \frac{\boxed{13 - 9}}{2} + 6$$

- Combine terms by adding and subtracting from left to right.

$$(4) \cdot 2^2 - \frac{4}{2} + 6$$

Circle the remaining terms:

$$\boxed{(4) \cdot 2^2} \; \boxed{\tfrac{4}{2}} + \boxed{6}$$

Simplify *within* circled terms using the Order of Operations as above:

$$\boxed{4 \cdot 2 \cdot 2} \; \boxed{\tfrac{4}{2}} + \boxed{6}$$

$$16 - 2 + 6$$

$$20$$

NAMING ALGEBRA TILES

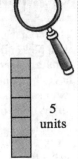

Algebra tiles help us represent unknown quantities in a concrete way. For example, in contrast to a 1×5 tile that has a length of 5 units, like the one shown at right, an x-tile has an unknown length. You can represent its length with a symbol or letter (like x) that represents a number, called a variable. Because its length is not fixed, the x-tile could be 6 units, 5 units, 0.37 units, or any other number of units long.

5 units

1 unit

x

1 unit

←Can be any length→

Algebra tiles can be used to build algebraic expressions. The three main algebra tiles are shown at right. The large square has a side of length x units. Its area is x^2 square units, so it is referred to as an x^2-tile.

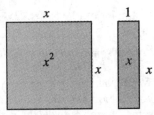

The rectangle has length of x units and width of 1 unit. Its area is x square units, so it is called an x-tile.

The small square has a side of length 1 unit. Its area is 1 square unit, so it is called a one or unit tile. Note that the unit tile in this course will not be labeled with its area.

Notes:

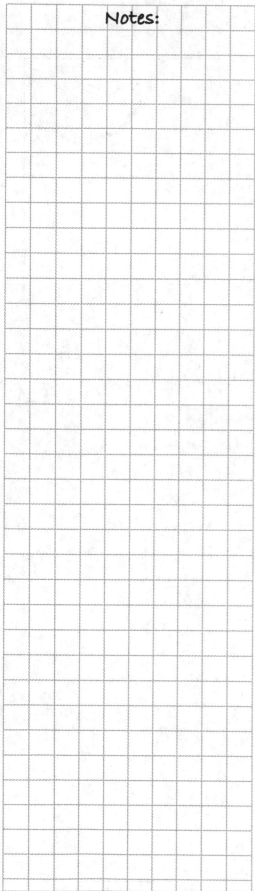

COMBINING LIKE TERMS

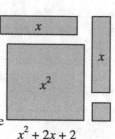

This course uses tiles to represent variables and single numbers (called **constant terms**). Combining tiles that have the same area to write a simpler expression is called **combining like terms**. See the example shown at right.

$$x^2 + 2x + 2$$

More formally, **like terms** are two or more terms that have the same variable(s), with the corresponding variable(s) raised to the same power.

Examples of like terms: $2x^2$ and $-5x^2$, $4ab$ and $3ab$.

Examples that are *not* like terms: 5 and $3x$, $5x$ and $7x^2$, a^2b and ab.

When you are not working with the actual tiles, it helps to visualize them in your mind. You can use the mental images to combine terms that are the same. Here are two examples:

Example 1: $2x^2 + x + 3 + x^2 + 5x + 2$ is equivalent to $3x^2 + 6x + 5$

Example 2: $3x^2 + 2x + 7 - 2x^2 - x + 7$ is equivalent to $x^2 + x + 14$

When several tiles are put together to form a more complicated figure, the area of the new figure is the sum of the areas of the individual pieces, and the perimeter is the sum of the lengths around the outside. Area and perimeter expressions can be **simplified**, or rewritten, by combining like terms.

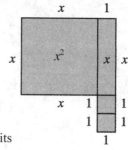

For the figure at right, the perimeter is:
$x + 1 + x + 1 + 1 + 1 + 1 + 1 + x + x = 4x + 6$ units

CHAPTER 7: RATES AND OPERATIONS

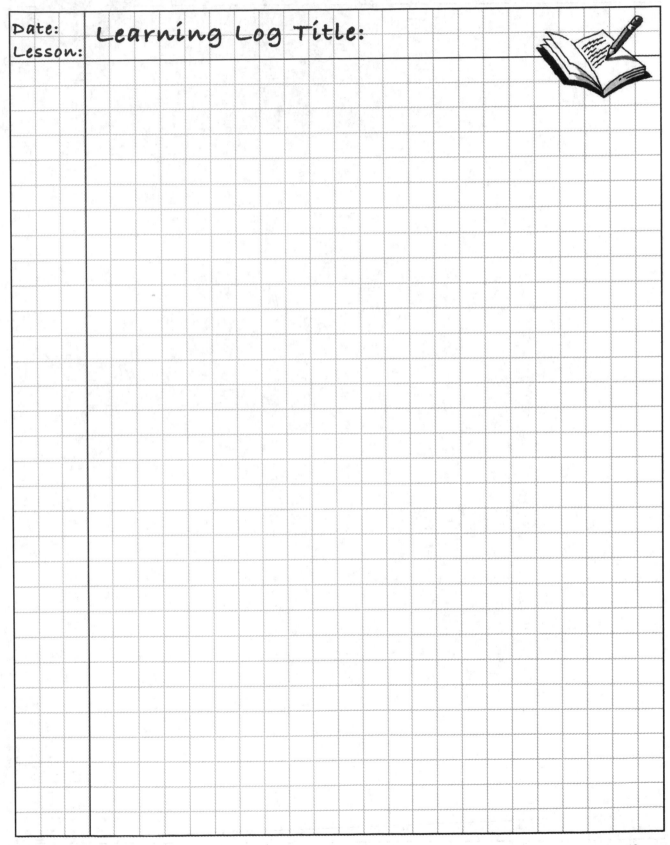

Date:
Lesson:

Learning Log Title:

Date:	Learning Log Title:
Lesson:	

| Date: | Learning Log Title: |
| Lesson: | |

| Date: | Learning Log Title: |
| Lesson: | |

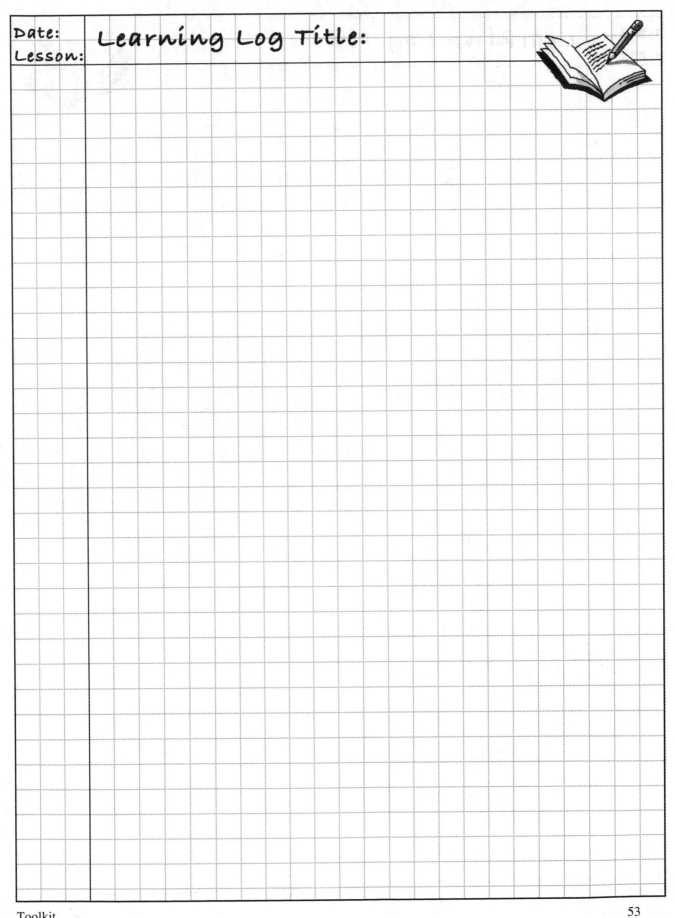

Date:
Lesson:

Learning Log Title:

Date:	Learning Log Title:
Lesson:	

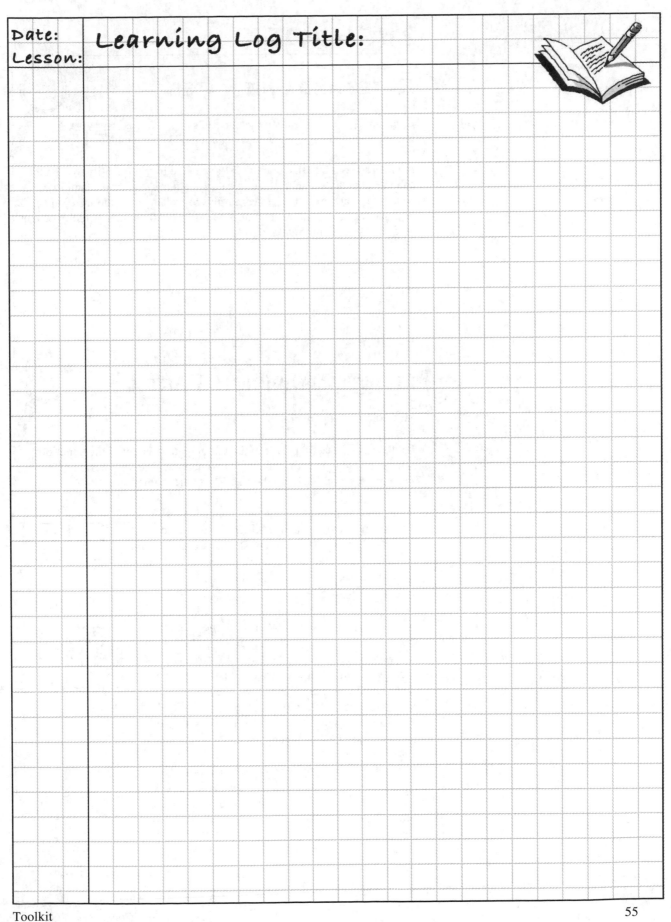

Date:
Lesson:

Learning Log Title:

MATH NOTES

RATES AND UNIT RATES

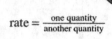

In Lesson 7.1.1, you learned that a **rate** is a ratio that compares two different quantities.

$$\text{rate} = \frac{\text{one quantity}}{\text{another quantity}}$$

A **unit rate** is a rate that compares the change in one quantity to a 1-unit change in another quantity. For example, *miles per hour* is a unit rate, because it compares the change in miles to a change of 1 hour. If an airplane flies 3000 miles in 5 hours and uses 6000 gallons of fuel, you can compute several unit rates.

It uses $\frac{6000 \text{ gallons}}{5 \text{ hours}} = 1200 \frac{\text{gallons}}{\text{hour}}$ or $\frac{6000 \text{ gallons}}{3000 \text{ miles}} = 2 \frac{\text{gallons}}{\text{mile}}$, and it travels at $\frac{3000 \text{ miles}}{5 \text{ hours}} = 600 \frac{\text{miles}}{\text{hour}}$.

FRACTION DIVISION, PART 1

Method 1: Using Diagrams

To divide by a fraction using a diagram, create a model of the situation using rectangles, a linear model, or another visual representation of it. Then break that model into the fractional parts named.

For example, to divide $\frac{7}{8} \div \frac{1}{2}$, you can draw the diagram at right to visualize how many $\frac{1}{2}$-sized pieces fit into $\frac{7}{8}$. The diagram shows that one $\frac{1}{2}$ fits one time, with $\frac{3}{8}$ of a whole left. Since $\frac{3}{8}$ is $\frac{3}{4}$ of $\frac{1}{2}$, you can see that $1\frac{3}{4}$ $\frac{1}{2}$-sized pieces fit into $\frac{7}{8}$, so $\frac{7}{8} \div \frac{1}{2} = 1\frac{3}{4}$.

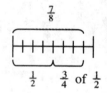

Alternately, you could think of $\frac{7}{8}$ as the quantity that you have and $\frac{1}{2}$ as the size of the group that you want, such as having $\frac{7}{8}$ ounce of chocolate and needing $\frac{1}{2}$ ounce for each cake recipe. How many cakes could you make? In this case the diagram at right might be useful. The diagram shows $\frac{7}{8}$ being divided into groups of $\frac{1}{2}$. The leftover $\frac{3}{8}$ ounce creates another $\frac{3}{4}$ of a group, so again, $\frac{7}{8} \div \frac{1}{2} = 1\frac{3}{4}$.

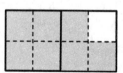

Method 2: Using Common Denominators

To divide a number by a fraction using common denominators, express both numbers as fractions with the same denominator. Then divide the first numerator by the second. An example is shown at right.

$$\frac{2}{5} \div \frac{3}{10} = \frac{4}{10} \div \frac{3}{10}$$
$$= 4 \div 3$$
$$= \frac{4}{3} = 1\frac{1}{3}$$

MULTIPLICATIVE INVERSES AND RECIPROCALS

Two numbers with a product of 1 are called **multiplicative inverses**.

$$\frac{8}{5} \cdot \frac{5}{8} = \frac{40}{40} = 1 \qquad 3\frac{1}{4} = \frac{13}{4}, \text{ so } 3\frac{1}{4} \cdot \frac{4}{13} = \frac{13}{4} \cdot \frac{4}{13} = \frac{52}{52} = 1 \qquad \frac{1}{7} \cdot 7 = 1$$

In general $a \cdot \frac{1}{a} = 1$ and $\frac{a}{b} \cdot \frac{b}{a} = 1$, where neither a nor b equals zero. Note that $\frac{1}{a}$ is the **reciprocal** of a and $\frac{b}{a}$ is the reciprocal of $\frac{a}{b}$. Also note that 0 has no reciprocal.

FRACTION DIVISION, PART 2

Method 3: Using a Super Giant One

To divide by a fraction using a Super Giant One, write the two numbers (dividend and divisor) as a complex fraction with the dividend as the numerator and the divisor as the denominator. Use the reciprocal of the complex fraction's denominator to create a Super Giant One. Then simplify, as shown in the following examples.

$$6 \div \frac{3}{4} = \frac{\frac{6}{1}}{\frac{3}{4}} \cdot \boxed{\frac{\frac{4}{3}}{\frac{4}{3}}} = \frac{\frac{6 \cdot 4}{1 \cdot 3}}{1} = \frac{6}{1} \cdot \frac{4}{3} = \frac{24}{3} = 8$$

$$\frac{3}{4} \div \frac{2}{5} = \frac{\frac{3}{4}}{\frac{2}{5}} \cdot \boxed{\frac{\frac{5}{2}}{\frac{5}{2}}} = \frac{\frac{3 \cdot 5}{4 \cdot 2}}{1} = \frac{3}{4} \cdot \frac{5}{2} = \frac{15}{8} = 1\frac{7}{8}$$

Method 4: Using the "Invert and Multiply" Method

Notice that the result of multiplying by the Super Giant One in the above examples is that the denominator of the complex fraction is always 1. The resulting numerator is the product of the first fraction (dividend) and the reciprocal of the second fraction (divisor).

To use the "Invert and Multiply" method, multiply the first fraction (dividend) by the reciprocal (multiplicative inverse) of the second fraction (divisor). If the first number is an integer, write it as a fraction over 1.

Here is the second problem from the examples above that was solved with the Invert and Multiply method:

$$\frac{3}{4} \div \frac{2}{5} = \frac{3}{4} \cdot \frac{5}{2} = \frac{15}{8} = 1\frac{7}{8}$$

Notes:

DISTRIBUTIVE PROPERTY WITH VARIABLES

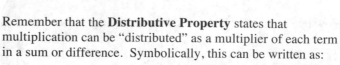

Remember that the **Distributive Property** states that multiplication can be "distributed" as a multiplier of each term in a sum or difference. Symbolically, this can be written as:

$$a(b + c) = ab + ac \quad \text{and} \quad a(b - c) = ab - ac$$

For example, the collection of tiles at right can be represented as 4 sets of $x + 3$, written as $4(x + 3)$. It can also be represented by 4 x-tiles and 12 unit tiles, written as $4x + 12$.

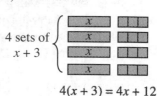

4 sets of
$x + 3$

$$4(x + 3) = 4x + 12$$

MATHEMATICS VOCABULARY

Variable: A letter or symbol that represents one or more numbers.

Expression: A combination of numbers, variables, and operation symbols. For example, $2x + 3(5 - 2x) + 8$. Also, $5 - 2x$ is a smaller expression within the larger expression.

Term: Parts of the expression separated by addition and subtraction. For example, in the expression $2x + 3(5 - 2x) + 8$, the three terms are $2x$, $3(5 - 2x)$, and 8. The expression $5 - 2x$ has two terms, 5 and $2x$.

Coefficient: The numerical part of a term. In the expression $2x + 3(5 - 2x) + 8$, for example, 2 is the coefficient of $2x$. In the expression $7x - 15x^2$, both 7 and 15 are coefficients.

Constant term: A number that is not multiplied by a variable. In the expression $2x + 3(5 - 2x) + 8$, the number 8 is a constant term. The number 3 is not a constant term, because it is multiplied by a variable inside the parentheses.

Factor: Part of a multiplication expression. In the expression $3(5 - 2x)$, 3 and $5 - 2x$ are factors.

SOLVING AND GRAPHING INEQUALITIES

An **equation** always has an equal sign. An **inequality** has a mathematical inequality (comparison) symbol in it. To **solve** an equation or inequality means to find all the values of the variable that make the equation true. See the examples below.

Solve this equation:
$$x + 3 = 7$$
The solution is:
$$x = 4$$

Solve this inequality:
$$x - 2 < 5$$
The solution is:
$$x < 7$$

To solve and graph an inequality with one variable, first treat the problem as if it were an equality and solve the problem. The solution to the equality is called the **boundary point**. For example, to solve $x - 4 \geq 8$, solve $x - 4 = 8$. The solution $x = 12$ is the boundary point for the inequality $x - 4 \geq 8$.

Since the original inequality is true when $x = 12$, place your boundary point on the number line as a solid point. Then test one value on either side in the *original* inequality to determine which set of numbers makes the inequality true. This is shown with the examples of $x = 8$ and $x = 15$ at right. After testing you can see that the solution is $x \geq 12$.

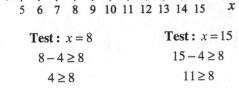

Test : $x = 8$
$$8 - 4 \geq 8$$
$$4 \geq 8$$
FALSE!

Test : $x = 15$
$$15 - 4 \geq 8$$
$$11 \geq 8$$
TRUE!

When the inequality is $<$ or $>$, the boundary point is *not* included in the answer. On a number line, this would be indicated with an open circle at the boundary point. For example, the graph of $x < 7$ is shown below.

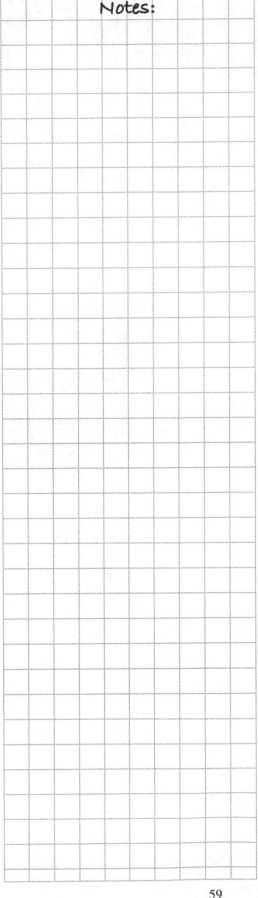

CHAPTER 8: STATISTICS AND MULTIPLICATION EQUATIONS

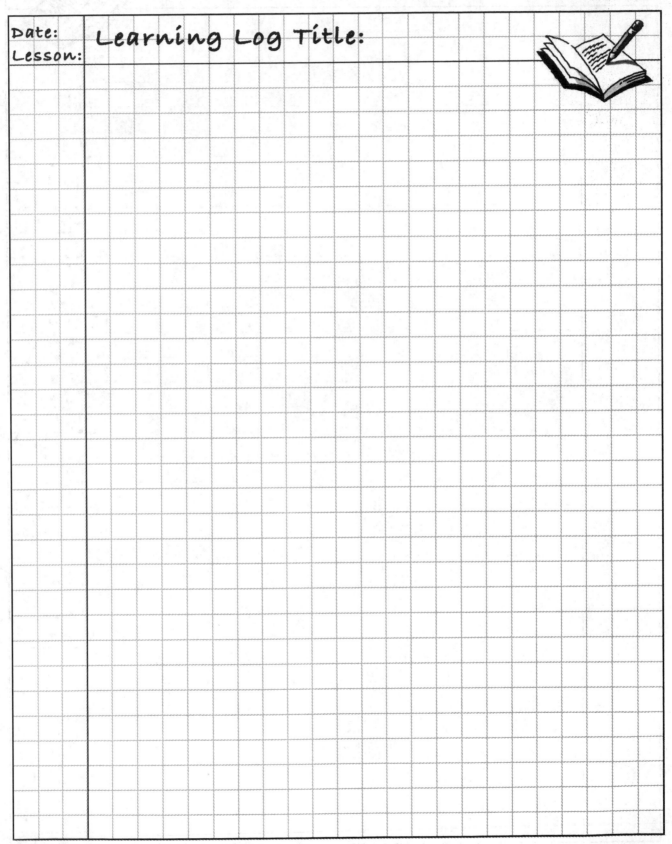

Date:
Lesson:

Learning Log Title:

Date:	Learning Log Title:
Lesson:	

Date: Lesson:	Learning Log Title:

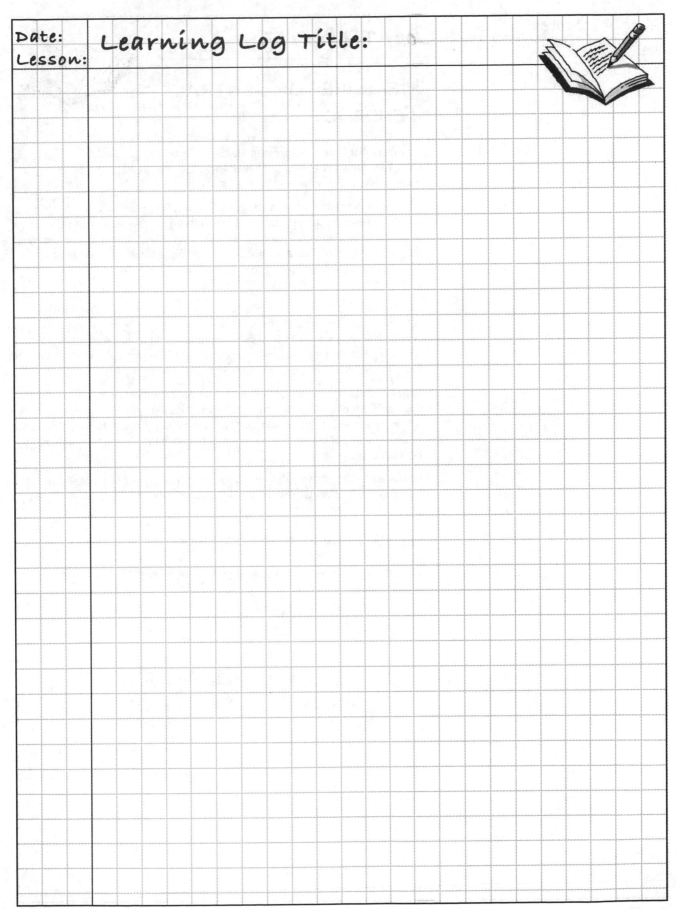

MATH NOTES

MEASURES OF CENTRAL TENDENCY

Numbers that locate or approximate the "center" of a set of data are called the **measures of central tendency**. The mean and the median are measures of central tendency.

The **mean** is the arithmetic average of the data set. One way to compute the mean is to add the data elements and then to divide the sum by the number of items of data. The mean is generally the best measure of central tendency to use when the set of data does not contain **outliers** (numbers that are much larger or smaller than most of the others). This means that the data is symmetric and not skewed.

The **median** is the middle number in a set of data arranged numerically. If there is an even number of values, the median is the average (mean) of the two middle numbers. The median is more accurate than the mean as a measure of central tendency when there are outliers in the data set or when the data is either not symmetric or skewed.

When dealing with measures of central tendency, it is often useful to consider the distribution of the data. For symmetric distributions with no outliers, the mean can represent the middle, or "typical" value, of the data well. However, in the presence of outliers or non-symmetrical distributions, the median may be a better measure.

Examples: Suppose the following data set represents the number of home runs hit by the best seven players on a Major League Baseball team:

$$16, 26, 21, 9, 13, 15, 9$$

The mean is $\frac{16+26+21+9+13+15+9}{7} = \frac{109}{7} \approx 15.57$.

The median is 15, since, when arranged in order (9, 9, 13, 15, 16, 21, 26), the middle number is 15.

MEAN ABSOLUTE DEVIATION

One method for measuring the spread (variability) in a set of
data is to calculate the average distance each data point is from the
mean. This distance is called the **mean absolute deviation**. Since
the calculation is based on the mean, it is best to use this measure of
spread when the distribution is symmetric.

For example, the points shown below left are not spread very far from the
mean. There is not a lot of variability. The points have a small average
distance from the mean, and therefore a small **mean absolute deviation**.

The points above right are spread far from the mean. There is more
variability. They have a large average distance from the mean, and
therefore a large mean absolute deviation.

QUARTILES AND INTERQUARTILE RANGE (IQR)

Quartiles are points that divide a data set into four equal parts (and
thus, the use of the prefix "quar" as in "quarter"). One of these points is
the median, since it marks the middle of the data set. In addition, there
are two other quartiles in the middle of the lower and upper halves: the
first quartile and the **third quartile**.

Suppose you have this data set: 22, 43, 14, 7, 2, 32, 9, 36, and 12.

To find quartiles, the data set must be placed in order from smallest to
largest. Then divide the data set into two halves by finding the median of
the entire data set. Next, find the median of the lower and upper halves of
the data set. (Note that if there is an odd number of data values, the
median is not included in either half of the data set.) See the example
below.

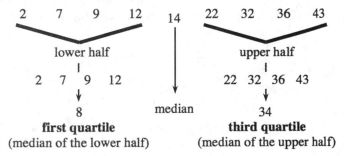

Along with range and mean absolute deviation, the **interquartile range**
(IQR) is a way (to measure the spread of the data. Statisticians often
prefer using the IQR to measure spread because it is not affected much by
outliers or non-symmetrical distributions. The IQR is the range of the
middle 50% of the data. It is calculated by subtracting the first quartile
from the third quartile. In this case, the IQR is 34 − 8, or IQR = 26.

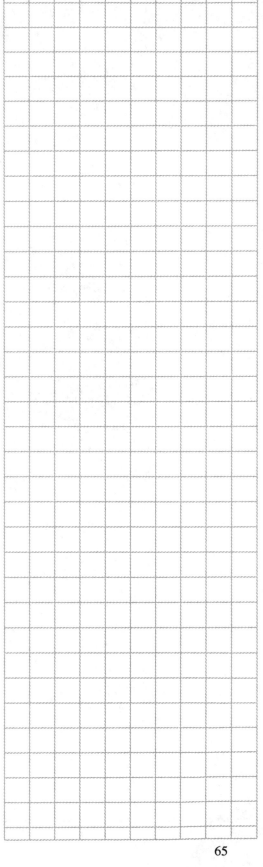

Notes:

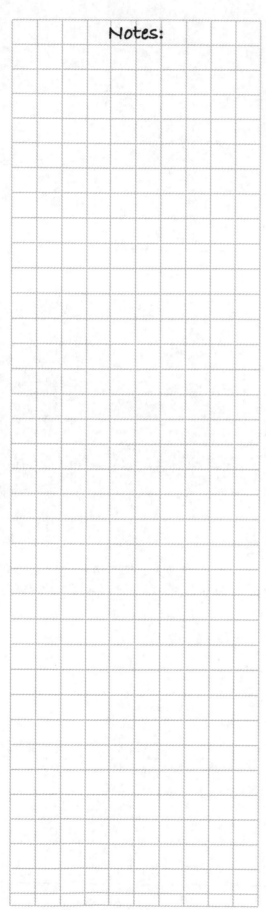

Notes:

BOX PLOTS

A **box plot** (also known as a "box-and-whiskers" plot) displays a summary of data using the median, quartiles, and extremes of the data. The box contains "the middle half" of the data. The right segment represents the top 25% of the data, and the left segment represents the bottom 25% of the data. A box plot makes it easy to see where the data are spread out and where they are concentrated. The larger the box, the more the data are spread out.

To construct a box plot using a number line that shows the range of the data, draw vertical line segments above the median, first quartile and third quartile. Then connect the lines from the first and third quartiles to form a rectangle. Place a vertical line segment above the number line at the maximum (highest) and minimum (lowest) data values. Connect the minimum value to the first quartile and the maximum value to the third quartile using horizontal segments. For the data set used in the Quartile Math Note, namely, 2, 7, 9, 12, 14, 22, 32, 36, and 43, the box plot is shown below.

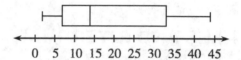

DISTANCE, RATE, AND TIME

Distance (d) equals the product of the **rate** (or **speed**) (r) and the **time** (t). This is usually written as $d = r \cdot t$. The units of distance (such as feet or miles) and units of time (such as seconds or hours) are used to write the units of rate (feet per second or miles per hour). The equation can also be written in the equivalent forms of $r = \frac{d}{t}$ and $t = \frac{d}{r}$.

One way to make sense of this relationship is to treat rate as a unit rate that equals the distance covered in one hour (or minute) of travel. Then $r \cdot t$ is t sets of r lengths, which is rt long. For example, if someone travels for 3 hours at 5 miles per hour, you could represent this situation by the diagram below.

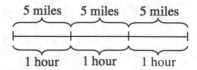

You can also use the same equation to find either rate or time if you know the other two variables. For example, if you need to travel 200 miles and need to be there in 4 hours, you have the equation $r \frac{\text{mi.}}{\text{hr.}} = \frac{200 \text{ mi.}}{4 \text{ hrs.}}$, so $r = 50 \frac{\text{mi.}}{\text{hr.}}$.

EQUIVALENT MEASURES

When you need to compare quantities, it is often helpful to write them using the same units. Here are some common units of measurement and their relationships:

Length	Volume	Weight
12 inches = 1 foot	8 ounces = 1 cup	16 ounces = 1 pound
36 inches = 1 yard	16 ounces = 1 pint	2000 pounds = 1 ton
3 feet = 1 yard	2 pints = 1 quart	
5280 feet = 1 mile	4 quarts = 1 gallon	

Time
60 seconds = 1 minute   24 hours = 1 day

60 minutes = 1 hour   7 days = 1 week

One year is closely approximated as 365.25 days, or a bit more than 52 weeks and 1 day. Two commonly used approximations based on these figures are:

365 days ≈ 1 year   52 weeks ≈ 1 year

Notes:

CHAPTER 9: VOLUME AND PERCENTS

Date: Lesson:	Learning Log Title:	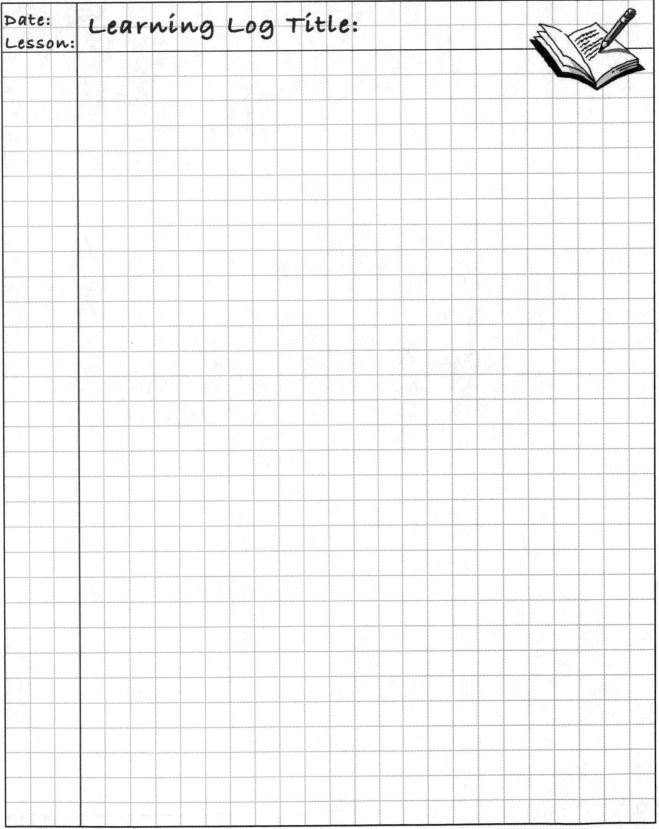

Date:	Learning Log Title:
Lesson:	

Date: Lesson:	Learning Log Title: 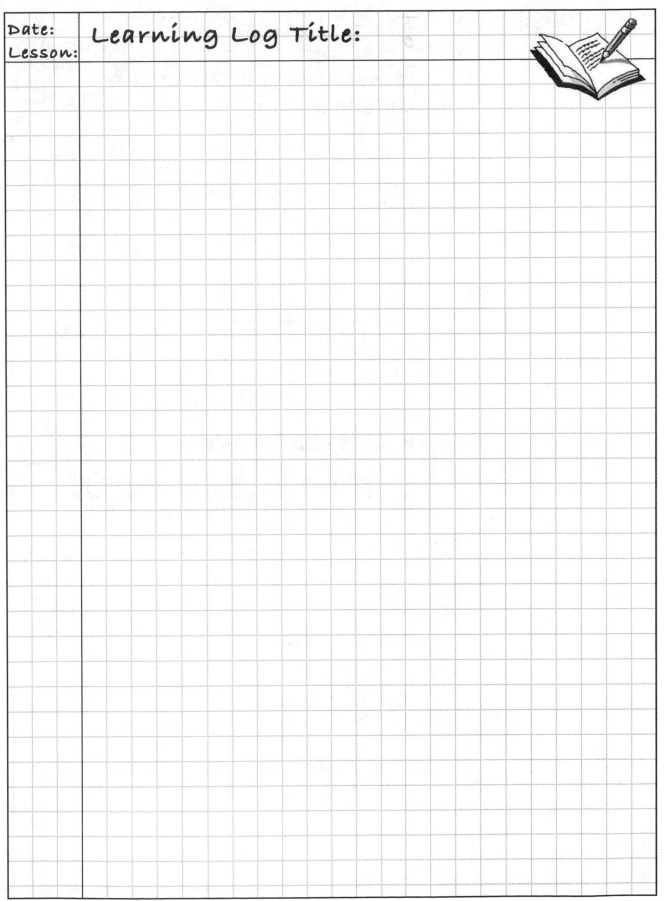

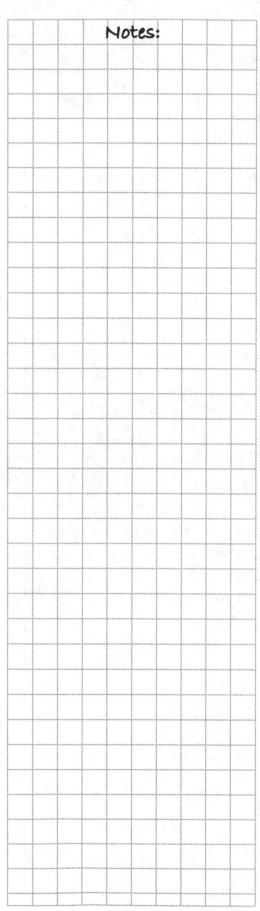

MATH NOTES

MEASUREMENT IN DIFFERENT DIMENSIONS

Measurements of **length** are measurements in **one dimension**. They are labeled as cm, ft, km, etc.

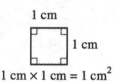

1 centimeter

Measurements of **area** are measurements in **two dimensions**. They are labeled as cm^2, ft^2, or, square centimeters, square feet, etc. The abbreviation "cm^2" is read as "square centimeters and *not* as "centimeters squared."

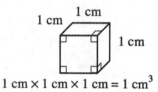

1 cm

1 cm

$1\ cm \times 1\ cm = 1\ cm^2$

Measurements of **volume** are measurements in **three dimensions**. They are labeled as cm^3, ft^3, or, cubic centimeters, cubic feet, etc. Read "ft^3" as "cubic feet" and *not* as "feet cubed."

1 cm   1 cm

1 cm

$1\ cm \times 1\ cm \times 1\ cm = 1\ cm^3$

PRISMS AND PYRAMIDS

Three-dimensional figures are those that have length, width, and height. The flat sides of the figure are called **faces**, and an **edge** is where two faces meet. The point where three or more sides meet is called a **vertex** (plural: vertices).

A **prism** is a special kind of solid with flat faces, called a **polyhedron**. It has two parallel faces that are the same shape and size called **bases**. The other faces (called **lateral faces**) are parallelograms (or rectangles). No holes are permitted in the solid.

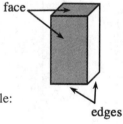

face

edges

A prism is named for the shape of its base. For example:

triangular prism

pentagonal prism

A **pyramid** is a three-dimensional figure with a base that is a polygon. The lateral faces are formed by connecting each vertex of the base to a single point (the vertex of the pyramid) that is above or below the surface that contains the base.

vertex

base

VOLUME OF A PRISM

The **volume** of a prism is a measure of how many unit cubes exactly fill it. To calculate the volume, multiply the number of cubes in one layer by the number of layers it takes to fill the shape. Since the volume of one layer is the area of the base (B) multiplied by 1 (the height of that layer), you can use the formula below to compute the volume of a prism.

If h = height of the prism, V = (area of base) · (height)
$$V = Bh$$

Example:

Area of base = (2 in.)(3 in.) = 6 in.^{2}

(Area of base)(height) = (6 in.^{2})(4 in.) = 24 in.^{3}

Volume = 24 in.^{3}

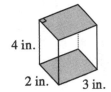

4 in.

2 in.   3 in.

SURFACE AREA

Surface area is a measure of the number of unit squares that completely wrap around a shape. The surface area of a prism or pyramid is the sum of the areas of each of the faces, including the bases. Surface area is expressed in square units.

A **net** is a drawing of each of the faces of a prism or pyramid, as if it were cut along its edges and flattened out. A net can be helpful to see the different area subproblems that need to be solved to find the total surface area. There are usually several ways to make a net of a prism or pyramid. One example for each solid is shown below.

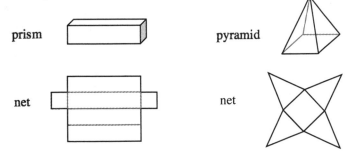

prism

net

pyramid

net

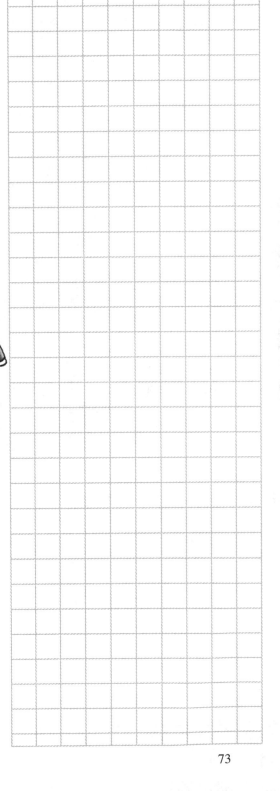

Notes:

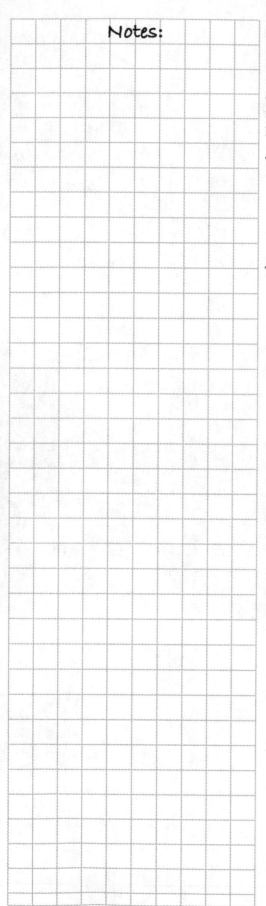

Notes:

CALCULATING PERCENTS BY COMPOSITION

Calculating 10% of a number and 1% of a number will help you calculate other percents **by composition**.

$$10\% = \frac{1}{10}$$
$$1\% = \frac{1}{100}$$

To calculate 13% of 25, you can think of 10% of 25 + 3(1% of 25).

$$10\% \text{ of } 25 \Rightarrow \frac{1}{10} \text{ of } 25 = 2.5 \text{ and}$$

$$1\% \text{ of } 25 \Rightarrow \frac{1}{100} \text{ of } 25 = 0.25 \text{ so}$$

$$13\% \text{ of } 25 \Rightarrow 2.5 + 3(0.25) \Rightarrow 2.5 + 0.75 = 3.25$$

To calculate 19% of 4500, you can think of 2(10% of 4500) − 1% of 4500.

$$10\% \text{ of } 4500 \Rightarrow \frac{1}{10} \text{ of } 4500 = 450 \text{ and}$$

$$1\% \text{ of } 4500 \Rightarrow \frac{1}{100} \text{ of } 4500 = 45 \text{ so}$$

$$19\% \text{ of } 4500 \Rightarrow 2(450) - 45 \Rightarrow 900 - 45 = 855$$

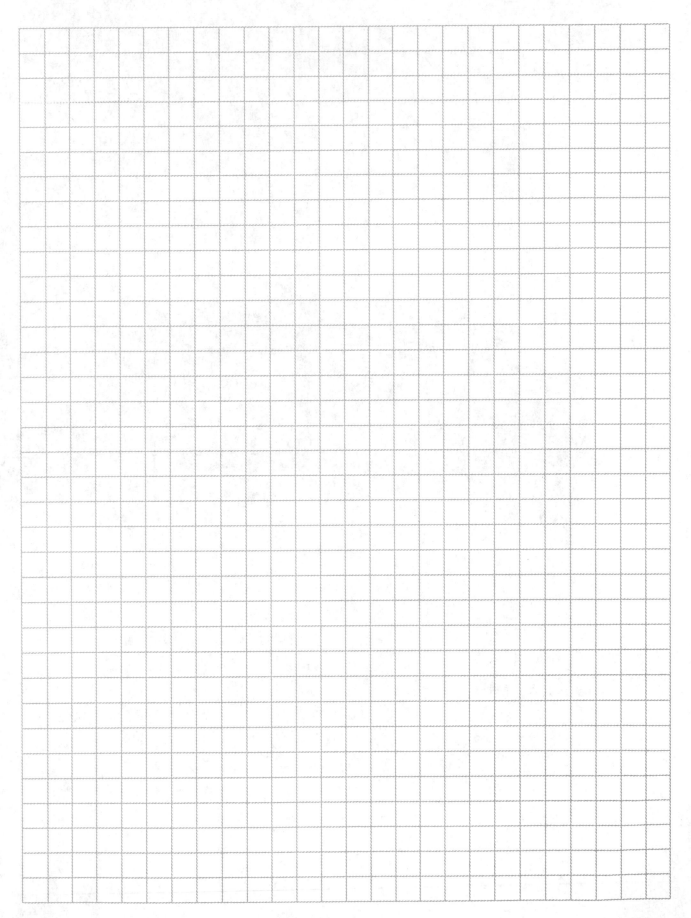

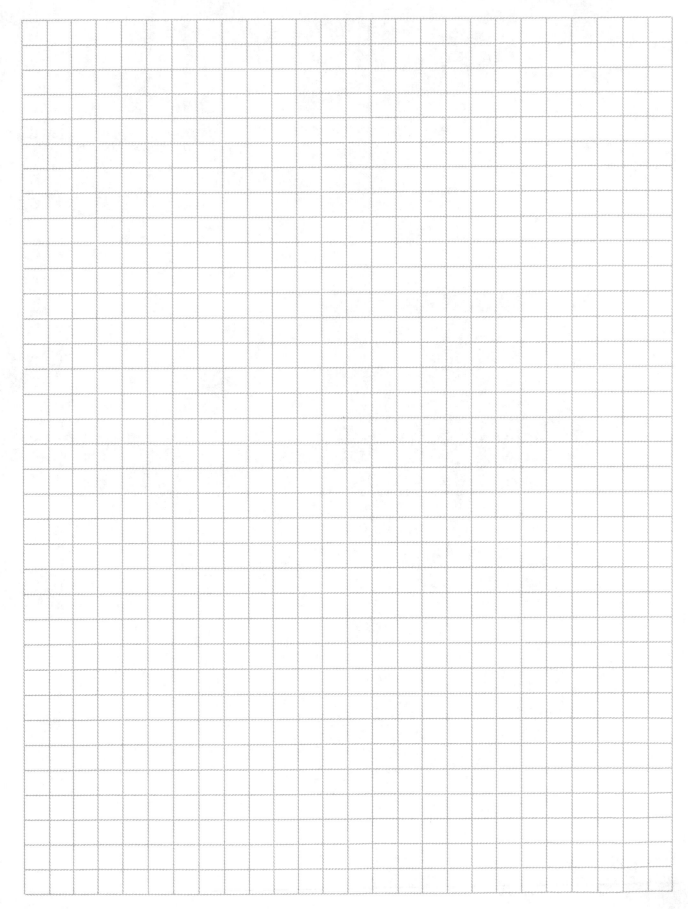

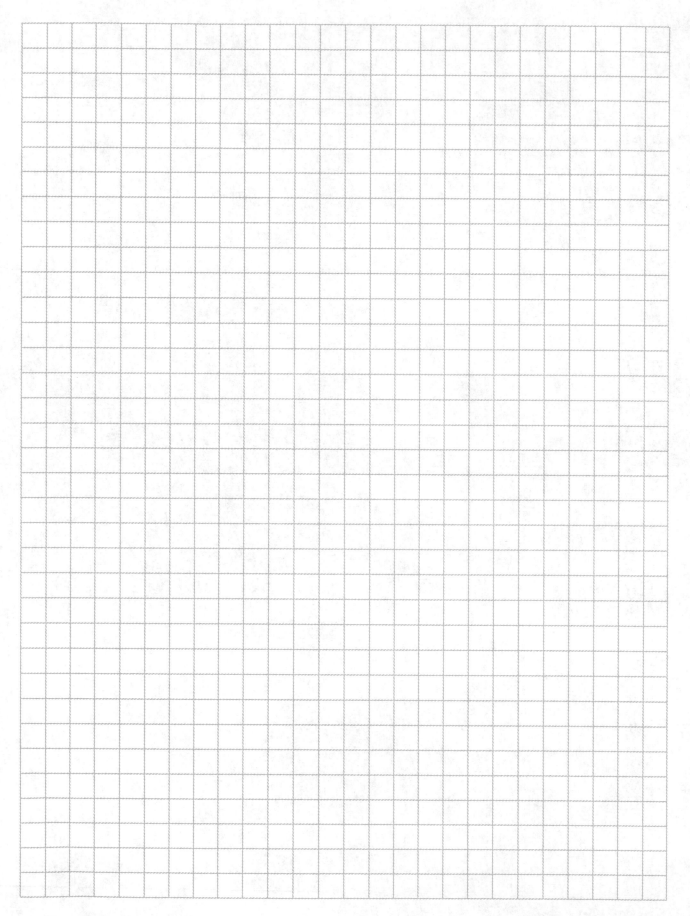

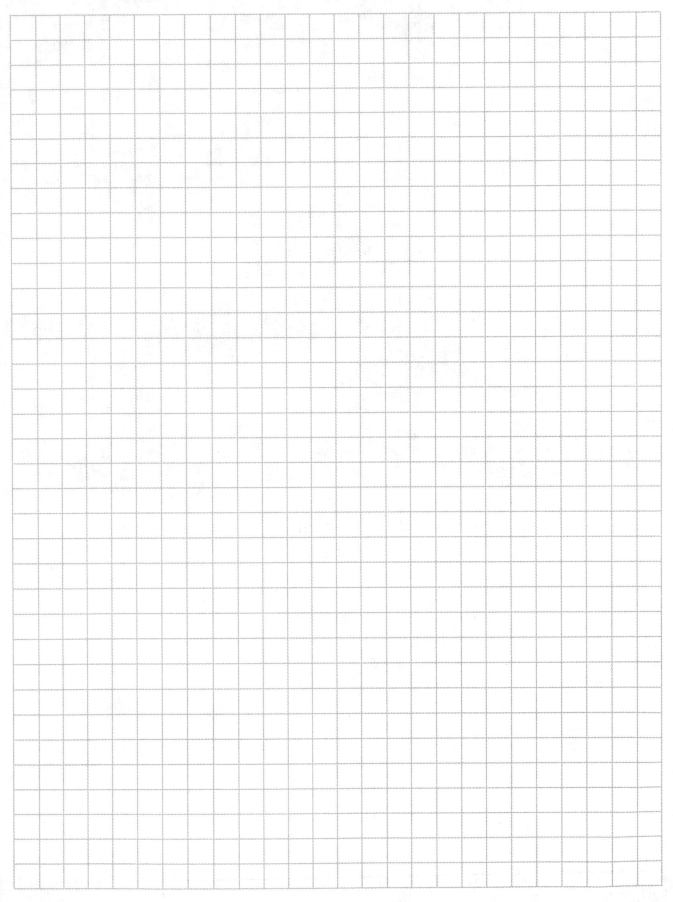

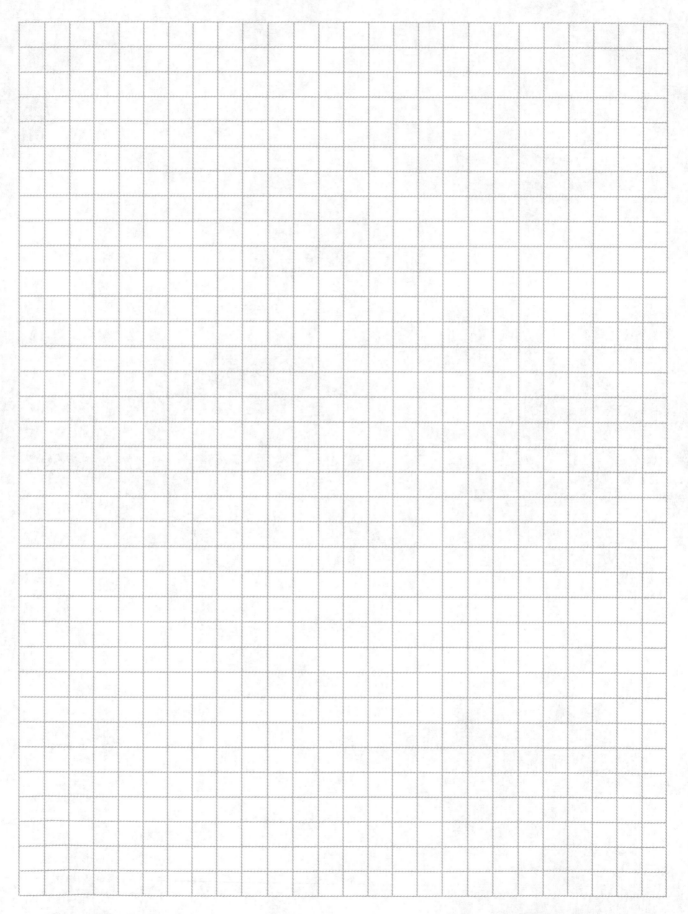

Index

A

Absolute value, 25
Addition
    of fractions, 21
    of integers, 24
Additive inverse, 24
Algebra tiles, 47
Algebraic expression, 32, 47
    evaluating, 32
Area, 4, 13, 72
    conservation of, 39
    parallelogram, 39
    trapezoid, 46
    triangle, 39
    units for, 13, 14
Area model for multiplication, 37
Average, 64

B

Bar graph, 12
Base
    of a parallelogram, 39
    of a prism, 72
    of a rectangle, 38
    of a triangle, 39
Boundary point, 59
Box plot, 66

C

Coefficient, 58
Combining like terms, 48
Complex fraction, 57
Composite number, 6
Composition, to calculate percents, 74
Conjecture, 5
Conservation of area, 39
Constant term, 48, 58
Coordinate, 23
Counting number, 6

D

Data analysis, 64
Data display
    bar graph, 12
    box plot, 66
    dot plot, 12
    histogram, 12
    stem-and-leaf plot, 13
    Venn diagram, 12
Decimal
    as a fraction, 22
    as a percent, 22
    division, 57
    multiplication, 38
    place value, 4
Denominator, 21, 30, 37
Dimensions, 72
Discrete, 12
Distance, 66
    between parallel lines, 39
    perpendicular, 39
Distributive Property, 15, 58
Division
    long, 30
    of decimals, 57
    of fractions, 56
        standard algorithm, 57
Dot plot, 12

E

Edge, 72
Equation, 59
Equivalent units of measure, 69
Evaluate an expression, 32
Even number, 6
Exponent, 46
Expression, 58
    algebraic, 47
    evaluating, 32

F

Face, 72, 73
    lateral, 72
Factor, 6, 58
    greatest common, 15
First quartile, 65, 66

O

Odd number, 6
Opposite, 23
   addition, 24
Order of Operations, 46
Ordered pair, 23
Origin, 23
Outlier, 64

P

Parallel, 39
Parallelogram, 39
Percent, 21
   as a decimal, 22, 39
   as a fraction, 22, 39
   calculating by composition, 74
Perimeter, 4
Perpendicular, 39
Place value, 4
Plane, 39
Plane figures, 13
Point, 23
   boundary, 59
Polyhedron, 72
Positive number(s), 24
Prime number, 6
Prism, 72
   base, 72
   surface area, 73
   volume, 73
Property, Distributive, 15
Pyramid, 72
   surface area, 73

Q

Quadrilateral
   parallelogram, 39
   rectangle, 4
Quartile, 66

R

Range, interquartile, 65
Rate, 66
   of change, 56
   unit, 56
Ratio, 32
   rate of change, 56
Reciprocal, 57

Rectangle, 4, 38
   area, 4
   base, 38
   height, 38
Representations of a Portion web, 22
Rewriting fractions, 21, 31
Rounding, 5

S

Simplify, 48
Solve, 59
Speed, 66
Spread, 65
Square unit, 14
Standard algorithm
   fraction division, 57
Stem-and-leaf plot, 13
Substitution, 32
Subtraction of fractions, 21
Super Giant One, 57
   dividing fractions, 57
Surface area
   of a prism, 73
   of a pyramid, 73
Symbols, comparison, 6
Symmetric data distribution, 65

T

Term(s), 32, 58
   like, 48
Third quartile, 65, 66
Three-dimensional, 72
Time, 66
Trapezoid, 46
Triangle, 39

U

Unit rate, 56
Units of measure
   for area, 14

V
Variability, 65
Variable, 31, 47
Variable expression, 32
Venn diagram, 12
Vertex, 72
Volume, 72
  of a prism, 73

W
Web
  Representations of a portion, 22

X
x-axis, 23
x-coordinate, 23

Y
y-axis, 23
y-coordinate, 23